GERMAN EXPRESS LOCOMOTIVES

GERMAN EXPRESS LOCOMOTIVES

ANDREAS KNIPPING

PEN & SWORD TRANSPORT

AN IMPRINT OF PEN & SWORD BOOKS LTD.
YORKSHIRE – PHILADELPHIA

Originally published by GeraMond Verlag GmbH in 2020 as
Die deutschen Schnellzug-Dampflokomotiven

First published in Great Britain in 2022 by
Pen & Sword Transport
An imprint of
Pen & Sword Books Ltd
Yorkshire - Philadelphia

ISBN 978 1 52679 574 8

Typeset in Palatino by SJmagic DESIGN SERVICES, India.
Printed and bound in the UK by CPI (UK) Ltd.

Pen & Sword Books Ltd. incorporates the Imprints of Pen & Sword
Archaeology, Atlas, Aviation, Battleground, Discovery, Family History,
History, Maritime, Military, Naval, Politics, Railways, Select, Transport,
True Crime, Fiction, Frontline Books, Leo Cooper, Praetorian Press,
Seaforth Publishing, Wharncliffe and White Owl.

For a complete list of Pen & Sword titles please contact

PEN & SWORD BOOKS LIMITED
47 Church Street, Barnsley, South Yorkshire, S70 2AS, England
E-mail: enquiries@pen-and-sword.co.uk
Website: www.pen-and-sword.co.uk

or

PEN AND SWORD BOOKS
1950 Lawrence Rd, Havertown, PA 19083, USA
E-mail: uspen-and-sword@casematepublishers.com
Website: www.penandswordbooks.com

CONTENTS

FOREWORD

Inter-zonal traffic
The Erfurt 01.05s were responsible for the inter-zonal traffic from Berlin to Bebra until 1973. 01 0520 is seen here leaving the Hönebach Tunnel a few miles west of the border between East and West Germany. (*Andreas Knipping*)

In May 1968 my mother and I were invited to a confirmation celebration at Genthin on the line from Berlin to Magdeburg. It was still taken for granted then that the night inter-zonal trains from Regensburg to Hof would be hauled by an 01 Pacific. When I opened the window, I was treated to a great display of thundering exhaust smoke and flying sparks. After the family celebration in Genthin, we walked back through the sleeping town to my grandmother's apartment, where we were all staying as usual. The level crossing gates across the post office road were, as nearly always, closed. It was coming up to midnight. I had watched numerous trains at the crossing on previous occasions, but will never forget the visual and acoustic flashes of swirling red, gleaming black and roaring exhaust of an 01 and its sleeping cars on its way from Berlin to Helmstedt, as it broke the stillness and darkness of the street.

Such memories from my childhood and youth accompany my travels, photography, collecting and writing about the railway from then until the threshold of old age. As with many railway enthusiasts, express steam locomotives have always held a very special place for me.

It is my privilege and honour to be able to tell their condensed history here. It is not a challenge for me to celebrate in words and pictures the last decades of the surviving classes of steam traction, but rather it is an opportunity to awaken an understanding of the history of the development of these well-known designs.

Andreas Knipping

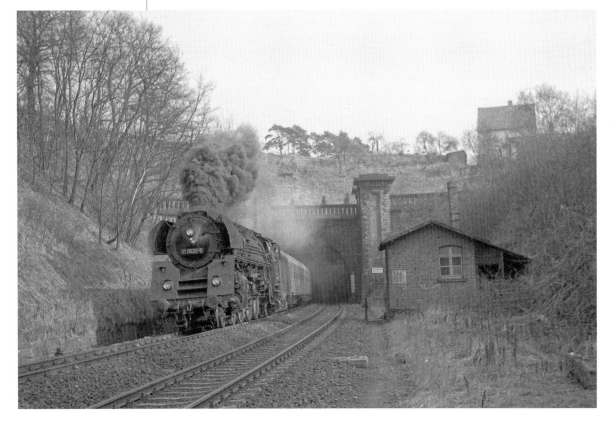

Note: The wheel and axle arrangements of all four coupled and other locomotives are described in the original German text as 2'B or 2'C1. To save space and make it more readable for English language readers, they are written here as 4-4-0s or 4-6-2s.

Chapter 1

MOVING AWAY FROM NARROW-GAUGE RAILWAYS

From coal trains to express journeys by rail

'We fly away on narrow iron rails…' This line from an 1848 poem reminds one of the unexpected explosion of greater mobility. Developed for the transport of coal and minerals, the flexible new transport system of the railway bloomed quickly into the business of carrying passengers. The expanding universe of factories, mines, blast furnaces and ports, and their supply chains of banks, stock markets, business houses, interest societies and seats of learning, required more and more businessmen, engineers, bankers, civil servants, lawyers, academics and journalists to make long journeys across the country between hometowns, factories, mines, banks, universities and news publishers, or between influential gentlemen's clubs and the stately homes of the nobility.

Also completely new was the mass appearance of the sons of families from Regensburg, Poznan, Koblenz or Linz leaving their country villages and estates for their new career opportunities – and

perhaps also their wives – far away in the pulsating centres of Essen, Szczecin, Mannheim, Hamburg, Nuremberg, Ostrava or Katowice. Then there were family visits to baptisms, confirmations, weddings, birthdays or communal Christmases, not to mention the funeral of a beloved relative, where economic travel was an important factor. Thus long journeys took their place in the emotional episodes of life as well as the necessities of career and work.

In addition to health considerations, emotional reasons were also a good motivation for travel in large numbers, namely to take holidays in rural idylls, whose attraction was only enhanced with the threat of the industrial age. With the unavoidable increase of noise and smoke in the towns, these holiday journeys acquired important social, health and political functions. Much too late, it was not until the second half of the twentieth century that they became available en masse to the working classes. A serious aspect of this ability to make long journeys was

access to health spas and sanatoria in the fresh air of the hills and countryside. Before the effective treatment of tuberculosis with antibiotics became possible in the 1950s, the medical profession knew no other remedy than sending the patient who had contracted the disease for a month or even year-long therapy in the forests and clean air. The construction of corresponding sanatoria and the sending of workers there was one of the socio-political achievements of

Black gold
Coal stood at the beginning of the existence of all railways. Without the black gold from the depths of England, northern France, the Ruhr, the Saar and Upper Silesia, our ancestors could not have travelled on railways, built locomotives or driven any trains. (*Franz Ullmann*)

Postage stamps

The Deutsche Eisenbahn-Versicherungskasse, originally founded as a self-organising cartel from German railway insurance offices, was active in the field of postage stamps, which have been completely forgotten about today. The stamp showing the famous *Adler* of 1835 was followed by a much enlarged 2-2-2 for local and express passenger trains, although by 1870 the design had already reached its peak.

Named after its founder

When Borsig built its first 2-2-2 in 1844 with the name *Beuth* for the Berlin – Anhalter Railway, the evolution into separating the express, slow passenger and goods locomotive classes had not yet flourished. However, the basic layout of cylinders, motion and driving wheels remained a stable part of locomotive construction for the next century and a half. (*Andreas Knipping*)

the imperial era. Admittedly, a large number of the patients still died in Beelitz, Brilon Wald or Clausthal-Zellerfeld, or in the magical mountains of Switzerland.

The post or courier carriages naturally matured gradually to two or three axle coaches, although for a long time the railway companies stuck to the basic structure of placing old coach bodies over the general running gear. The coach bodies were constructed as an integral design, glazed, and upholstered, and were covered overhead with a tar-soaked canvas. The passenger space became compartmentalised with doors only leading to the outside. Small stoves provided warmth in winter. In the time of a rigidly strict class society, members of the nobility, ministers, diplomats, generals or even ladies of rank travelling alone did not

wish to travel with sinister fellow travellers such as non-commissioned officers, salesmen, cheeky upstarts from engineering schools or curious newspaper writers. Significantly, classless travel with an open-car plan was common from the start in the republican-minded USA. Being confined to a compartment also required frequent and often longer intermediate train stops. People wanted to be served a meal in a station restaurant at lunchtime and, finally of course, calls of nature also had to be satisfied. The early express trains were lit by candles or oil lamps – a very weak light shining over us from the past age.

Let us now look at the locomotives that were needed for the ever faster journey through decades of society's increasing mobility.

The definition of the express locomotive: large diameter wheels!

In order to obtain the needed working speeds, faster locomotives had to be provided with larger driving wheels. Therefore, the 'high-wheeled' express locomotive had to be differentiated from the small-wheeled goods and branch line locomotives, as well as the middle-sized diameter wheels of local passenger locomotives. The dividing line in Europe for express locomotives was reliably set at 1.8 metres (approximately 6ft).

Given the maximum axle load on the rails and the physical limits of friction between wheels and rail, each increase in size and weight and increase in tractive effort required the load to be distributed over more and more axles. The designer had to determine the permissible axle load and therefore the number of axles needed, depending on the train weights and gradient profile of the route and necessary adhesion. Ideally, the entire weight of the locomotive would have been used for adhesion, but a basic problem of the steam locomotive was that the weight of the boiler, motion and other parts added many more tons over and above the necessary adhesion weight. This meant that there was inevitably 'dead weight' on the non-driving wheels of the engine and tender.

Old steam locomotive systems
Serious research into the history of the locomotive is older than railway photography. These pencil drawings record the chronology of locomotives of the Royal Prussian Eastern Railway which operated between Berlin, Königsberg and the Russian border. On the upper left is No.36, built by Borsig in 1853, a typical 2-4-0 with 6ft diameter driving wheels. There was still no footplate cab and the crew had to stand outside in the open in all weathers. Further down, on the bottom left, is the Borsig 104–108, a 2-2-2 from 1857 with 6ft 6in diameter driving wheels.

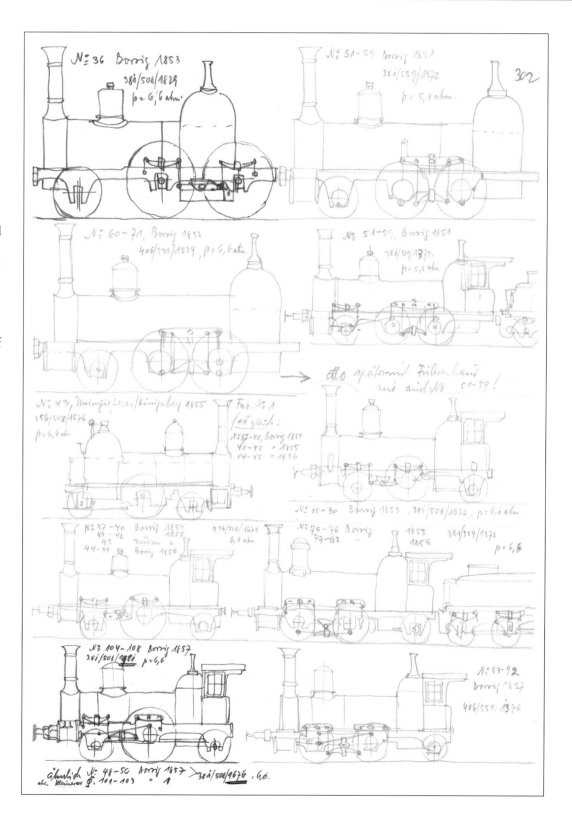

Keyword: The customer

In Germany, express steam locomotives were initially procured in great numbers by private railway companies in the north and west. These railways were the:

Aachen – Düsseldorf – Ruhr
Aachen – Maastricht
Altona (Hamburg) – Kiel
Bergisch – Mark (Westphalia)
Berlin – Anhalt
Berlin – Dresden
Berlin – Hamburg
Berlin – Potsdam – Magdeburg
Berlin – Stettin
Brunswick
Breslau – Warsaw
Cologne – Minden

Frankfurt – Bebra
Frankfurt – Hanau
Halle – Kassel
Magdeburg – Halberstadt
Magdeburg – Leipzig
Magdeburg – Wittenberg
Nassau
Lower Silesia – Mark
Upper Silesia
Rhein
Saarbrück
Schleswig

Stargard – Posen
Thuringian & Westphalian
Hanover State
Hesse Ludwig
Main – Neckar
Main – Weser
Royal Eastern
Oder Right Bank
Rhein Suburban
Lower Schleswig Branch
Taunus
Wilhelm

Those railway companies with more than 50 express locomotives were:
The Hanover State Railway (114)
The Bergisch – Mark Railway (106 out of a total fleet of 963)
The Upper Silesian Railway (101)
The Royal Eastern Railway (73)
The Berlin – Anhalt Railway (68)
The Lower Silesia – Mark Railway (68 out of a total fleet of 869)
The Cologne – Minden Railway (67)
The Berlin – Potsdam – Magdeburg Railway (57)
The Rhein Railway (52)

It is no surprise that the extreme boom in the second half of the imperial era in the particularly economically dynamic Prussia, extending from the Saarland coal mines to the Upper Silesian collieries and the steelmaking industries of the Ruhr and Aachen, and from Berlin to east Prussia, led to the prolific procurement of locomotives in these areas. Between 1879 and 1904 the north German private railway companies were nationalised to form the Royal Prussian Railway Company (KPEV), which was then the largest railway administration in the world. In the south, the history of the railways was very different. Apart from a few exceptions in Bavaria and Saxony, the availability of private capital was missing here. From the beginning, state railways existed in Baden, Bavaria, Saxony and Württemberg. Between 1920 and 1938, the only private system outside the German State Railway (Deutsche Reichsbahn – DR) with express passenger trains was the Lübeck – Büchen Railway. The Reichsbahn kept its name after 1945 in the German Democratic Republic (DDR – East Germany) and also in the allied zones around Berlin. After 1949, in the Federal Republic of Germany (BRD – West Germany), it operated as the German Federal Railway (Deutche Bundesbahn – DB).

COMPANY OWNERS OF EXPRESS LOCOMOTIVES

Company	Number
Railways in north and west Germany taken over by the KPEV	1,181
KPEV (Royal Prussian Railway)	3,456
Bavarian Eastern Railway	30
Royal Bavarian State Railway (including Bavarian designs built in DR epoch)	570
Royal Saxony State Railway	267
Pfalz (Palatinate) Railway	89
Lübeck – Büchen Railway	22
Royal Württemberg State Railway	174
Archduke of Baden State Railway	243
German State Railway (DR)	571
German Federal Railway (DB)	2
Total	**6,602**

Chapter 2

CREATIVE WHEEL ARRANGEMENTS

from 2-2-2 to the world-wide successful 4-4-0

From the steam locomotive to the 2-2-2

The English, who at the beginning of the nineteenth century were the first to put the steam engine on rails in mines and other industrial sites, were also the first to build the simple four-wheeled steam 'carriages'. Initial concerns about the lack of adhesion with narrow wheels on smooth rails turned out to be unfounded. The mathematical tangential meeting point between the circular wheel surface and the horizontal rail is in reality so small – hardly visible to the eye – and permanently on the move. The impetus of the wheel movement will overcome the lack of adhesion, and the wheel arrangements of 0-2-2 and 2-2-0 were born. There was soon dissatisfaction with the riding of such locomotives, and from 1833 the leading and load-bearing functions of the small diameter wheels were separated from the driving function of the large diameter wheels, with the driving wheels now fitted between the two smaller wheel sets. Stephenson had thereby created a patent for the 2-2-2 wheel arrangement. It soon proved to be extraordinarily capable of further development and was consequently enlarged and improved over the following decades. Germany's first locomotive, the *Adler* (Eagle), was delivered in 1835 for the Nuremberg – Fürth Railway and belonged to this type of locomotive. Almost every European railway company between 1835 and around 1870 initially exclusively procured 2-2-2 locomotives, and continued to use them to a considerable extent in later years. When, from 1850 onwards, a division of the initial mixed service into faster long-distance work, local passenger and goods activities emerged, the former of these remained the domain of the 2-2-2, meaning the first express locomotives of the world had this wheel arrangement.

Problems of the long-boilered 2-2-2

In order to increase the performance of the locomotives, the thermal value of the coal needed to be better used. It was thus essential to lengthen the initially short pipes with a longer boiler to gain more space and time for the outflowing gasses to pass over the surrounding water. As with many other innovations, it was George Stephenson who dared to significantly lengthen the tubes in the 2-2-2, from 9ft to 13ft, for example, and later to as much as 14ft.

The lengthening of the boiler naturally led to parts of it overhanging the wheels on both ends: the cylinder block and smokebox at the front, and the raised boiler at the rear above the three-axle running gear. This type of construction, with its established poor characteristics, was known as the 'long-boiler' in the history of engineering.

On a test run in England in 1845, a long-boiler 2-2-2 toppled

The Saxon *Gustav Harkort*
Only a few 2-2-2s were still active when live short exposure photography was possible. The *Gustav Harkort* of the Royal Saxon State Railway was built in 1856 and was in service until 1902. The cab was added at a later date.

and derailed at 48mph. On 21 January 1851, a long-boilered 2-2-2 derailed near Gütersloh on the Cologne – Minden Railway with a train in which the Prussian Crown Prince Frederick William, later Kaiser Frederick III, was travelling. The accident caused three fatalities and numerous injuries. This experience and following tests resulted in a general ban on the use of long-boilered machines on fast trains. The railways

managed to rebuild many of the locomotives fairly quickly, namely by positioning the rear trailing wheels behind the boiler. To the astonishment of all, the positioning of the rear axle further back from around 9½ft from the rear driving wheel to 14–15ft caused no issues, even on curved track, and even improved the smoothness of the ride. The winner in the Prussian companies was a 4-2-0 of the Crampton type, which ran at 70mph

without any trouble. The 2-2-2 moved from the long-boiler version with the rear axle now behind the boiler, with outside valve gear and correctly balanced cylinders. Before train weights rose considerably in the last third of the nineteenth century, this type of express locomotive worked well, and the same applied to local and stopping passenger locomotives with driving wheels between 5ft and 5ft 9in in diameter.

The Jubilee locomotive
Proud workers accompany the 1,000th locomotive built by Borsig in 1858, a 2-2-2 with 6ft 6in diameter wheels for the Cologne – Minden Railway. Locomotive construction at this time was still hand-crafted and not yet mechanised.

The Saxon veteran *Boehlen*
This picture of the former Saxon *Boehlen* (1858–1901) illustrates an important example of express locomotives of the time. In a departure from the long boiler design, the rear running axle has already been moved behind the raised boiler. Above the firebox is the dome, which was later recognised as being unproductive in terms of heat efficiency. In order to display the locomotive in a museum, the cab has been removed and the astonishing working conditions of those early days reconstructed.

The Bavarian standard
Other dimensions were required for regional state railways with significant gradients. The class AV from 1853 had driving wheels of only 5ft 6in in diameter, specifically designed for express trains in Bavaria.

LARGE DIAMETER WHEELED 2-2-2s BUILT	
Operator and manufacturer	**Number**
The later nationalised engines (KPEV) of the north and west German private railways by Borsig, Egestorff, Gute Hoffnungshütte Sterkrade, Henschel, Karlsruhe, Kessler, Ruffer, Schichau, Stephenson, Vulcan, the Dortmund Workshops of the Cologne – Minden Railway and Wöhlert, 1838 – 1875	288
The Royal Saxon State Railway by Hartmann and Borsig, 1856 – 1868	31
The Bavarian Eastern Railway by Maffei	12
The Archduke's Baden State Railway by Kessler, Meyer, Hartmann and Stephenson, 1844 – 1848 (for 5ft 3in broad gauge, later rebuilt to standard gauge)	31
Operational until about 1895	

LARGE DIAMETER WHEELED 4-2-0s BUILT	
Operator and manufacturer	**Number**
The later nationalised engines (KPEV) of the north and west German private railways by Borsig, Egestorff, Esslingen, Karlsruhe and Wöhlert, 1852 – 1856	78
Archduke's Baden State Railway by MBG Karsruhe, and HW Karlsruhe, 1854 – 1864	29
Palatinate Railway by Maffei and Esslingen, 1853 – 1864	18
Bavarian Eastern Railway by Maffei, 1857 – 1858	12
Operational until about 1890	

A Crampton in the Bavarian Palatinate
The Palatinate Railway's *Maxburg*, built in 1855 by the Karlsruhe Workshops, already had a relatively usable driver's cab in its later years of operation, but it had already been withdrawn by 1872.

Crampton's 4-2-0

The previously described 'long-boiler' problems and the initial dogma of the lowest possible axle weight were the reasons behind an idiosyncratic design. The Englishman Thomas Russell Crampton (1816 – 1888) placed both carrying axles at the front and the driving wheels behind the boiler. By doing this he was able to place the boiler in a deeper position. At the same time, it was possible to work with the recommended long driving rods without the cylinder overhanging the front. A disadvantage of the Crampton

design was that the largest element of the locomotive's weight was on these forward axles, with only a small part of the driving axle running under the footplate. For trains up to 100 tons, however, the Crampton engines performed well, and their development meant a further step in the progress of the express locomotive.

As the 2-2-2 type matured from mixed traffic to express work, so the 4-2-0 became the first type chosen exclusively for express passenger service in the history of international locomotives. In 1842 the first example even reached

75mph on a test run in England. The Crampton was used by several German railways between Bavaria and East Prussia, but its greatest use was in France. From the 1860s onwards, the gradual increase in train weights meant the star of the single-wheelers, as well as the Cramptons, began to wane. A significant step forward for the Cramptons was a simple flat cover over the firebox and ashpan area, continuing along the curved surface of the long boiler and thus removing the dome that had previously been built over the firebox.

The *Phoenix* becomes a museum locomotive
The two front axles of the Crampton locomotive gave good riding properties, however the weight on three axles gave lower adhesion. The Baden Railway's *Phoenix* from 1863 had been rebuilt from an earlier 2-2-2. Only a few engines built in later years came close to the driving wheel diameter of 7ft.

A jewel from Maffei in Munich
Die Pfalz, built in 1853 by Maffei, was operationally restored in 1925 using original parts from withdrawn machines and today belongs to the collection at the German Railway Historical Society's museum in Neustadt an der Weinstrasse.

A rarity: the 4-2-2

Only on the British private railway companies did the 2-2-2 develop into the 4-2-2 wheel arrangement, with the diameter of the single driving wheel increasing to an incredible 8ft. In 1896 the Royal Bavarian State Railway ordered a 4-2-2 with an additional special feature between the leading pair of wheels and the driving wheels: a booster with wheels only the size of the carrying wheels. The separate motion for this axle was only activated when starting up or on inclines, before being raised for normal running on the flat and faster stretches of the line. Like so many innovations that are interesting in principle, this '4-2-2-2' failed because it was too complicated, and in 1907 it was rebuilt as a 4-4-0.

The classic 2-4-0

Very shortly after the decision to go for three-axle locomotives with the 2-2-2 wheel arrangement, the idea of replacing one of the carrying pair of wheels with an additional driven axle arose, thus the 2-4-0 and 0-4-2 wheel arrangements came into being. The first useable locomotive built in Germany was the *Saxonia* of 1838, which was already an 0-4-2.

Locomotives of this wheel arrangement were built in Germany up to the 1870s, but were not suited for high speeds due to their large wheels at the front.

Hardly any wheel arrangement, however, was implemented more often, witnessed more experiments in design and found more universal use than the 2-4-0. Almost everywhere in the world they were used as either small-wheeled goods engines, local passenger engines with medium sized wheels, or, of particular interest in this case, as large diameter-wheeled express locomotives. An exception, however, was the USA, where from the earliest times a two-axle layout had been used for the driving wheels. The American 'island' in Germany was the state of Württemberg. Here, the 4-4-0 arrangement found favour (even if mostly with bogies with a fixed pivot) until a new engineering master in the 1860s took a step backwards to the 2-4-0, and consequently almost all 4-4-0s were rebuilt as 2-4-0s. As with the 2-2-2s, the early 2-4-0s suffered the same long-boiler problems and as no one yet dared to place the lead running wheels ahead of the cylinders, the smokebox hung over the front axle, as well as the boiler at the back.

Krauss' 4-2-2-2
The ingeniously conceived Bavarian 4-2-2-2 was built in 1896 by the firm Krauss. A 'booster' with small wheels for starting and steep gradients had the disadvantage of low adhesion, with only one pair of driving wheels on the rail. It was rebuilt as a 4-4-0 as early as 1907.

***Above*: Express trains to Upper Silesia**
In 1867 Borsig built this 2-4-0 with a driving wheel diameter of 6ft 2½in for the Upper Silesian Railway. The former high dome over the firebox has metamorphosed into a massive, vaulted dome in the centre of the boiler. The balance weights in the driving wheels have been applied in a primitive way and will later be incorporated into the body of the wheel in a sickle-shaped format.

***Left*: Men and their model**
The 2-4-0 shown in this model lacks the precise dimensions of the driving wheels of an express locomotive. However, the typical construction of a German steam engine from around 1860 can clearly be seen.

There remained a lack of clarity about many basic technical questions for almost all types of the 2-2-2, 2-4-0 and 0-4-2. It was believed at first that in the interest of ride stability, the locomotive frames must be placed outside the wheel sets, while the out-of-phase thrusts of the pistons only seemed controllable if they were operating close to one another between the wheels. However, from about 1845, outside valve gear and motion prevailed in Germany. For most countries, however, the inside gear remained dominant, meaning generations of train crews and shed staff suffered unfavourable working conditions as they prepared and oiled the locomotive for work.

The *Spree* from Chemnitz
The beauty of the original justifies including a local passenger locomotive with the same wheel arrangement as the 2-4-0 express engines, even though its 5ft-diameter wheels were smaller than its large-wheeled sisters. The Saxon State Railway's *Spree* was built by Hartmann of Chemnitz in 1856.

A 2-4-0 with an ancient boiler
According to today's knowledge, both the curved casing over the firebox and ashpan, as well as the large steam dome on this 2-4-0 from 1872, are too big. It also has too many boiler tubes and passages. This particular locomotive belonged to the Alsace-Lorraine Railway, which was part of the German Empire from 1871–1918 (before and after which time the territory belonged to France).

LARGE DIAMETER WHEELED 2-4-0s BUILT	
Operator and manufacturer	**Number**
The later nationalised engines (KPEV) of the north and west German private railways by Borsig, Carels, Egestorff, Hanomag, Hartmann, Heschel, Karlsruhe, Schichau, Schwartzkopf, Sigl, Strausberg, Union, Vulcan, Wilson & Wöhlert 1847 – 1890	785
KPEV (Royal Prussian Railway) by Borsig, BMAG, Henschel, Hanomag, Union, Schichau 1884 – 1898	274
Royal Bavarian State Railway by Maffei and Krauss 1874 – 1891	118
Palatinate Railway by Grafenstaden and Maffei, 1876 – 1884	15
Bavarian East Railway by Maffei, 1872	6
Royal Saxon State Railway by Hartmann, 1860 – 1890	55
Mecklenburg State Railway by Hartmann, 1864 – 1869 & 1879	20
Operational until about 1920	

the first coupled axle. The front pair of wheels were placed, as before, between the cylinders and driving wheel. As with the 2-2-2, after overcoming the early problems with the long-boiler, the improved 2-4-0 proved its worth not only as an express passenger locomotive, but also as a local passenger service for almost half a century, with the driving wheel diameter typically varying from 4ft 8in to 5ft 8in.

In order to understand and keep some sense of proportion, we must not overlook how the courier or postal express trains looked between 1850 and 1885. A train of two or three axle

Named after the master builder on the throne
The Palatinate Railway P 1 II built in 1876 by Grafenstaden shows off its 6ft 2in-diameter wheels under perfect lighting conditions. It bears the name of the immortal builder of monuments, the Bavarian King Ludwig I, and was withdrawn in 1912. (*Stephan Beständig Collection*)

In the 1840s the advance towards the extra axle began. For goods engines, the carrying wheels were dispensed with entirely as the whole weight of the engine was used for adhesion and the three-wheel coupling (0-6-0 arrangement) was used. Although outside the remit of this book, it should be noted that nearly every goods train in Europe rolled behind an 0-6-0 between 1850 and 1890.

The classic motive power for express trains in Germany from the middle of the nineteenth to the onset on the twentieth century was therefore the 2-4-0. The first example was built in 1852 by developing the 2-2-2 with a trailing wheel behind or under the firebox. Luckily, the higher pitch of the boiler in no way caused a loss of running stability, which was initially feared. The standard arrangement of outside horizontal cylinders was now the norm, almost without exception, and the drive came onto

Borsig's 291 for the Hanoverian State Railway

The Hanoverian State Railway ran between Rheine, Bremerhaven and Harburg (near Hamburg) in the north and Arenshausen and Münden (near Kassel) in the south. This express locomotive No.291, built by Borsig in 1869, proved to be thoroughly modern with its smooth, elongated and uncluttered shape. The cab is somewhat economical!

coaches was neither the length nor weight of two linked ICE coaches today. Speed seldom exceeded 45mph even if many of the locomotives could reach 60mph, and locomotive performance hardly reached more than 200 or 300 horsepower; no more than a powerful motorcar by today's standards.

Towards the end of the 2-4-0 era, engineers finally risked a design displaying a pair of carrying wheels far forward, and what is today more readily accepted as a more credible layout of the cylinders, motion and front driving wheel axle.

Germany in an express train compartment

Passengers eagerly embraced the developing railway environment; from its provincial coffee morning jaunts to countrywide long-distance travel, and for almost exactly 100 years it was the railway that captured the monopoly of this particular segment of the market.

The first steam train travelled merely a few kilometres in 1835, but by 1860 the thought of travelling over 60 miles without using a train was inconceivable, even if, in the beginning at least, the mesh-like network required part

of the journey to be undertaken on country roads.

By 1890, as the result of ever-increasing train weights, the 2-4-0 locomotive was seen less and less on both express and local train services. After a long period of stagnation, unprecedented economic growth returned, apart from a short period after the Second World War. If the industrial revolution based on coal and steel at the beginning of the nineteenth century had changed the world for ever, now the large-scale industrial use of chemical processes and electricity began. The population increased because

of the reduction of infant mortality, as well as the rapid improvement in diet and medical care. The pull to metropolitan areas occurred and European cities grew in size and structure, with many of these buildings and districts coveted today as part of a town's 'old quarter'. Urban tram electrical systems became partners to the steam driven railway, and thanks to large suburban areas being serviced by armies of nimble tank locomotives, local railway passenger traffic was able to reach new dimensions.

A 2-4-0 of the Pfalz (Palatinate) Railway
The *Hummel* ('Bumblebee') was basically very similar to the P 1 III class of the Palatinate Railway, built by Maffei in 1880 and in service until 1924. The Westinghouse air-brake pump between the wheel splashers was an addition in later years. Also note the hand-operated bell on the side of the cab.

Above: **A Bavarian express locomotive**
With 104 units produced, the B IX built
by Maffei in 1887 was the leading express
locomotive for the Royal Bavarian State
Railway in service on the right bank of the
Rhine for two decades. All the locomotives
still carried names, and one can only imagine
what the nameplate *Tittmoning* would fetch
on the collector's market today.

Left: **Faster through Saxony**
The Royal Saxon State Railway built the
express locomotive class VI b V compound
from 1886 to 1890. Seen here is the low-
pressure side on No.161, which remained in
service until 1924.

At the end of its active life
The Prussian management had a great deal of freedom in regards to their locomotive building programme, taking into consideration regional tradition and giving preference to local manufacturers. Between 1884 and 1887, the Royal Hanoverian State Railway (KED) acquired fourteen compound locomotives from Hanomag and Henschel with a conspicuously long-boiler, which were modernised with external Heusinger valve gear. The arrangement of the steampipes in a curved shape over the top of the boiler took some getting used to. Werner Hubert, the well-known classic railway photographer, came across this retired locomotive without its identification plates.

Of particular interest for this book is that in less than fifteen years, express trains developed from a half dozen rigid-axle carriages with stove heating and oil lamps to the express stock introduced in 1892 with six, eight or ten well-sprung bogie vehicles with air brakes, steam heating and gas lighting. A compromise was found between the large open carriages of American lineage and the compartment coaches, with six-seater compartments and through corridors. Curtains in the (rather rare) 1st class and (upholstered) 2nd class compartments provided protection and privacy from students, lower ranks of the army, foreign tourists, and those identified as social democrats, not to mention 3rd class passengers who found themselves in the corridors and side aisles that were provided to

Autopsy reveals the inner workings
The manufacturer's number 1,000 from 1874 was a B IX. It still exists today with its sectioned boiler barrel on display at 'Engineworld' in Freilassing. The boiler tubes and the steam line from the dome to the cylinders are clearly visible.

allow movement en route. En route to where? To the restaurant car, of course, another achievement of the express trains! The restaurant had now moved from the station to the train, meaning express trains themselves became a little town on wheels. Communication between coaches was guaranteed by gangway connections of pleated leather, popularly known as 'accordions', which gave protection from the wind and weather. It was therefore

attractive to be able to wander through the whole of the small town on wheels. Perhaps a middle-class daughter rather enjoyed standing at the open window of a side aisle in the 2nd class coach to see an officer candidate or young schoolteacher come out of the 3rd class coach, and maybe the land-owner from Pomerania would engage in conversation in the dining car with a grain merchant, even if he was, indeed, Jewish.

The evening version of the express train was a case all on its own, because now sleeping cars were becoming increasingly popular. While simple travellers could lean back and rest their heads, for better or worse, against the seat back or a hanging coat, or perhaps even lie across the bench in an empty compartment if they were in luck, the wealthier traveller could be attended to in the sleeping car, where there was a well-prepared bed ready and waiting for them, not to mention the modern facilities of a vanity unit and bedside lamp.

The traveller's wandering would finish at the back with the luggage van. There, if you had given the guard a tip, you could request him to keep an eye on your properly labelled luggage while you relaxed back in your compartment. It was even possible to find a caged pedigree dog in the luggage van.

Near the front of the train, between the locomotive and another luggage van, was the mail coach which, due to the intrinsic value of the items and matters of confidentiality, was closed off to the general public.

Otto von Bismarck, August Bebel, Matthias Erzberger, Kurt Eisner, Friedrich Ebert, Gustav Stresemann, Konrad Adenauer, Theodor Heuss and Kurt Schmacher, Marlene Dietrich, Claire Waldoff, Zarah

Leander and Hildegard Knef, Paul von Hindenburg, Erich Ludendorf or Wilhelm Groener, Thomas and Heinrich Mann, Karl Valentin, Gerthart Hauptmann, Kurt Tucholsky and Alfred Döblin, Max Schmeling, Willy Merkl or Sepp Herberger, Albert Einsten, Werner Heisenberg and Max Planck, Adolf Hitler, Joseph Goebbels, Hermann Göring and Heinrich Himmler, Gustav Mahler, Franz Werfel or

BX with Krauss-Helmholtz arrangement
An interesting transition appeared between the conventional B IX and the 4-4-0 of class B XI, when only fourteen examples of the B X were made between 1890 and 1891. They were already compound locomotives, with steam passing first to the high-pressure cylinders then to the low-pressure cylinder. Like all steam locomotives of the following decades, they had external Heusinger valve gear. Just as revolutionary was the combination of the leading carrying and coupled-axles with a Krauss-Helmholtz frame, a Bavarian invention that soon spread all over the world.

Alma Mahler-Werfel, Werner von Siemens, Walther Rathenau, Friedrich Krupp and Friedrich Flick, Karl Liebknecht, Rosa Luxemburg Ernst Thälmann, Wilhelm Pieck, Clara Zetkin and Walter Ulbricht, Hedwig Courths-Mahler, Käthe Kollwitz, Marie Juchacz and Sophie Scholl, Robert Koch, Sigmund Freud and Ferdinand Sauerbruch… Most of these men and women would never have met each other – and indeed many of them fought each other to the death – but what they all have in common is that on almost all of the long-haul journeys they made, whether in a luxurious or standard coach, they all sat behind a hard-working steam locomotive, an **express** steam locomotive. All young boys of the age knew and admired these machines, which were part of the golden age of the railway, and which embodied a piece of national pride thanks to the ingenuity of its engineers and the investment power of the German states.

***Opposite and left*: The final development of the 2-4-0**
The German 2-4-0 express locomotive found its final maturity – and also the beginning of the end – in the Prussian S 1 class. With 206 engines built between 1885 and 1898, the S 1 was allocated to the nationalised private railways in north Germany, replacing the decrepit and technically obsolete 2-2-2s, 4-2-0s and 2-4-0s. As a compound locomotive with topfeed water supply and sickle shaped wheel balance weights, it embodied modern construction principles and was capable of running at 55mph. Seen here is No.10 in three-quarter view, ready to depart from an unknown location. Also shown here is Magdeburg's No.29 at the platform, and lastly Stettin's No.8 on the turntable.

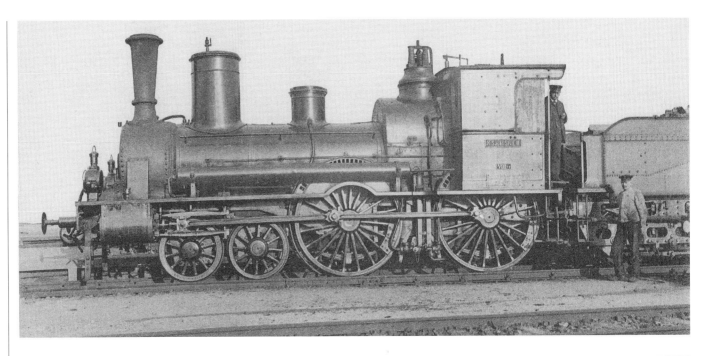

An Esslingen engine in Saxony

The Saxon VIII b I was an early 4-4-0 delivered in 1870, but for once was not built by Hartmann in its own state, but by Kessler in Esslingen. The extreme compressed arrangement of the bogie wheels did not help the running quality, but did improve the weight distribution. The long main air reservoir on both sides of the machine was another step forward, namely the provision of air brakes. Workshop photographs were possible from about 1860 by using a tripod and long exposures of a minute or more. Adequate shots of them in everyday service appeared after 1900. These rare images of the Saxon State Railway VIII b I are therefore of historical importance.

The Bavarian B XI
An example of the mature norm in German locomotive construction was the Bavarian B XI, with 39 two-cylinder and 100 compound engines being built between 1892 and 1900. The left side of compound locomotive 1265 is seen here with its voluminous low-pressure cylinder.

Victory of the 4-4-0

The increasingly popular 4-4-0 design, which was brought over from the USA, promised outstanding opportunities for development. The firebox, grate and ashpan could at last be brought easily between the coupled axles, and the long boiler could extend further forward, meaning the smokebox and boiler were in an ideal symmetry over the bogie. The locomotives were also more convincing visually, as the cylinders lay exactly between the pairs of bogie wheels and the chimney was often arranged exactly over the exhaust and blast pipes. With this lengthening of the axle arrangement compared with the layout of the 2-2-2 and 2-4-0, the rigid fixture of the front pair of wheels on the main frame was changed for ever more. Front and rear radial axles could be displaced sideways, whilst a bogie was provided with a displaceable pivot.

The difference it makes…
The arrangement of the valve gear and motion compared with a Saxon
VIII b I is demonstrated here by the slightly older Baden III a, built in 1869
by the Karlsruhe Engineering Works, which demonstrates a whole range of
contradicting construction principles. With its external frames and valve
gear, the firebox and grate area are no longer excessively heightened,
while the continuation of the cab on to the tender is an original feature.
(*Deutsches Museum, Munich*)

Inset: Look at this photograph of a modern Baden State Railway II a from
1888. Can you tell the difference from the III a? The carrying wheels are
set further apart and have the advantage of a better weight distribution,
while the springs of the coupled wheels are arranged under the axles. The
boiler has a higher pitch and, behind the Belgian Belpaire firebox, has a
horizontal roof.

A Baden 4-4-0 in the British style
The advance in design towards the end of the nineteenth and the beginning of the twentieth century was phenomenal. Shown here is a Baden State Railway 4-4-0, which appeared in 1892 as class II c, but looks fully emancipated in comparison with its four-year-older sister shown earlier. The boiler has almost doubled in volume (with 175lbs psi pressure instead of 100lbs psi) and is higher pitched; both front running wheels have been developed into a technically improved bogie; and the 6ft 11in-diameter driving wheels have given the machine a really elegant appearance. The valve gear has been placed inside the frames, thus following the British model.

Ideas about aerodynamics
The 'Windcutter' cab of the second variant of the Baden II c was as grotesque as it was useless. This and the covering of the smokebox to part the wind pressure experienced in running stimulated the thought process towards full streamlining in later years.

Experimental engine of the class S 2
After 1890, the Prussian management switched from 2-4-0s to 4-4-0s for all express traffic. Seen here is an experimental locomotive of class S 2 with internal gear at Berlin Anhalt station. In total 152 similar locomotives, though mostly two-cylinder engines, were built between 1890 and 1892. (*Werner Hubert*)

The new 4-4-0 two-cylinder compound engines, with their more efficient use of steam pressure, now became the standard design. In addition, the transition to the 4-4-0 coincided with other decisions that had great value for the entire future of the steam locomotive in Germany. Almost without exception, the frames were now placed on the inside, with the motion and Heusinger valve gear on the outside. However, a few railways and manufacturers in neighbouring Austria, France and Belgium went against these basic principles, at least up until the First World War. And with the externally unobtrusive Prussian S 4, technical history was written in 1898 with the first superheated steam engine in the world.

The building and further development of the 2-4-0 had taken roughly fifty years, but the boundary of the 4-4-0's development was visible within just ten years from the beginning of its triumphal march. Indeed, the number of its examples was never beaten: there were 1,027 Prussian S 3s alone, more than all the German Pacifics put together, and the following S 5 2 overtook the total of all German Atlantics built, with 367 engines. The superheated locomotives were further developed with feed-water heaters, but ever heavier and faster trains from the middle of the 1890s onwards required even newer solutions. The boiler, which could be carried on four axles, had insufficient reserves; and the two-axle driving wheels tended to slip more and more when accelerating and on inclines.

Unlucky locomotive
Engineers tried again and again to find subtle solutions to the lateral and upper part of the firebox at the rear of the boiler. One idea was to accommodate the firegrate within high-steam-pressure flexible pipes (ie, a water-tube firebox) that did not need stays. The fate of the experimental locomotive 341 *Cöln* in 1892 speaks for itself: on 6 March 1894 its boiler exploded.

With the Reichsbahn number
Most Bavarian B XIs lasted long enough
to receive German State Railway numbers.
Compound 1262, built in 1895, became 36 767.
Together with all the remaining B XIs, it was
withdrawn from service in 1931. (*Hermann Maey*)

Postmarked November 1903
This postcard from Fürth shows a typical
German express train at the turn of the century.
The B XI is followed by an ancient postal van, a
very modern bogie vehicle and two six-wheel
compartment coaches from the depths of the
nineteenth century.

The progressive B XI
A compound B XI seen from the driver's side. A steam pipe passes from the dome to the high-pressure cylinder. The passage from the high-pressure to low-pressure cylinder runs under the boiler. The number plate 1316 heralds further progress in the numbering of the machines: giving locomotives poetic names was virtually over by 1890.

Conversion from S 2 to S 3

External motion and valve gear finally relieved the strain of the crew's acrobatic practice of lubricating the internal gear and oiling points – except for multi-cylinder locomotives – and would remain the standard on the European continent forever. Seen here is a Prussian S 3, converted from an S 2, with an impressive 26½in diameter low-pressure cylinder.

Left: **In front of splendid architecture**
A wonderful picture postcard showing an S 3 shunting in Poznan. The sender posted it to an address in Grünberg, in Schleswig, after a visit to the 1911 exhibition. After the First World War Poznan no longer belonged to Germany, and after the Second World War neither did Grünberg; the results of German politics.

Below: **The great standard in Prussia: the S 3**
The Prussian S 3 commands great respect. With 1,027 units built between 1893 and 1904, it was the largest class of express locomotives in the world! This side view of 233 *Magdeburg* allows us to see its superior design. The steam exhaust system and smokebox are arranged symmetrically over the bogie, while the firebox, grate and ashpan are between the set of driving wheels.

S 3 in the sunlight

It is a stroke of luck to find 100-year-old photographs of locomotives in traffic. Here, slanting sunbeams perfectly showcase the contours of 213 Mainz, built in 1893. The rod from the cab to the equipment over the cylinder block regulated the supply of high-pressure steam to the low-pressure cylinder.

Through the streets of Hamburg

A much-photographed curiosity was the passing of the Cologne expresses through the busy streets of Hamburg before the rearrangement of its railway system in 1906. Here, an official with a red flag strides out in front of the slow moving S 3.

4-4-0s in Württemberg

Here is an older companion of the Prussian S 3 from Württemberg; an AD class built between 1899 and 1907, which although seven years younger is not exactly more modern in its design. Only the 6ft driving wheels indicate that it is an express locomotive. All the same, its boiler pressure of 200lbs psi exceeds the 175lbs psi that was used for an extended period by the Prussians. The two steam domes and connecting pipe brought no demonstrable thermal economic advantage.

***Above*: Saxon power**
Although three years older than the Württemberg AD, the Saxon VIII V I appears more powerful thanks to the dimensions of the boiler and the high- and low-pressure cylinders. The horizontal cover of the Belpaire firebox was by this time characteristic of the Saxon engines.

***Left*: Out and about near Hanover**
Coinciding with the enormous economic dynamism, especially in the north and west of Germany, at the turn of the century the Prussian Railway Company followed the S 3 with the more powerful S 5 2. The centre of the boiler was raised to a pitch of 8ft 2½in, compared with 7ft 5in of the S 3. The axle load of 8.2, 7.4, 11.7 and 11.7 tons on the four axles of the S 3 rose to 8.6, 8.7, 11.9 and 12.9 tons. Great effort was made to keep the increase in axle weight under control. It was still very rare in Germany that photographs were taken of trains out on the line, even into the 1920s. A high-quality camera with fast shutter speeds was needed, as well as strong sunlight and a relatively slow moving train, in order to capture S 5 2 No.535 *Hannover* in the region of Hanover in 1924, although here it is pictured with a stopping train, not an express, consisting of non-corridor compartment coaches. (*Rudolf Kreutzer*)

In the best light
With the Prussian S 5 2 we see a generation of locomotives that was representative of the motive power fleet of German railways. In beautiful, balanced light we see here 13 820 in 1930, shortly before its withdrawal. After two decades such four-coupled engines could no longer hold their own with the train weights offered, neither in express nor local passenger services.

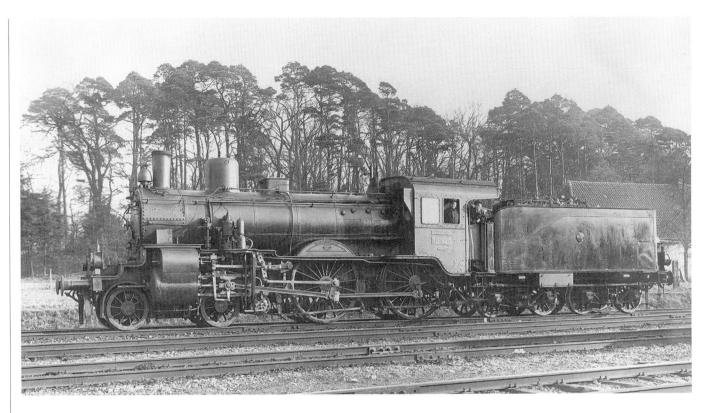

An engine of the Lübeck-Büchen Railway
In conjunction with the vast building developments of the greater Hamburg area, the last private railway in Germany (not to be confused with other constituted narrow-gauge railways), namely the Lübeck-Büchen Railway, was incorporated into the German State Railway in 1938. It had built seven examples of the S 5 2, of which just one came into the DR stock, receiving the distinguished number 13 001.

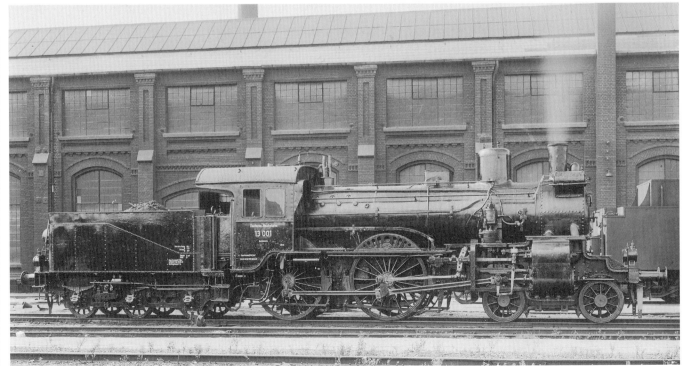

⁹/₄ gekuppelte Schnellzugs-Lokomotive S₅ der Preuss. Staatsbahn.
Erbaut von der Maschinenfabrik E. Schichau in Elbing 1908
Dienstgewicht 53300 kg, Geschwindigkeit 100 km.

Above: **In the time of the German State Railway**
This image shows 13 745 in active service with its driver and fireman.
Contrary to the state railway's usual official procedures, the number
plate has been replaced by a stencilled number on the cab side, which in
hindsight was rather realistic in view of its withdrawal as early as 1929.

Left: **Improved successor of the S 3**
Typical of the two-cylinder compound locomotives built between
1890 and 1905, such as the Prussian S 5 2 seen here, was the different
appearance of the engine's sides. Here we can see the high-pressure side
with the slimmer cylinder and the mechanism under the chimney for
feeding the low-pressure cylinder with high-pressure steam.

The caption on the images reads: Four-coupled express locomotive S 5 of
the Prussian State Railway.
Built by the E. Schichau Workshops in Elbing, 1908. Weight in service:
53.3 tons, maximum speed 62mph.

The world's first superheated steam locomotive

In 1897, the head of the Berlin rolling stock department, Robert Garbe (1847–1932), and the freelance engineer Wilhelm Schmidt (1828–1924) made engineering history in Kassel. They were successful in bringing about a practical application of the older, theoretical concept of superheating steam. We are all aware of the damp saturated steam of little more than 100°C from cooking at home, but these physicists realised that steam heated to 250–350°C would produce a much better performance. The final form of the superheater consisted of thin 'U' shaped tubes in which the steam collected in the dome would once again pass through the boiler tubes. The resultant S 4, based on the S 3 class, was the first superheated locomotive in the world.

Ancient history
A souvenir photograph of unknown railwaymen, the youngest of whom must have been dead for least seventy-five years. They are seen standing on the side of the bulky smokebox of the definitive S 4, beside the valve gear and motion. Note also the Borsig workplate on the wheel splasher.

A Bromberg S 4
One of the current lapses in railway literature is the fantasy that Germany gave existing locomotives to Poland as reparations after the First World War. However, if this S 4 was already based in the Bromberg district and the whole area was passed to the newly established Poland, then the fact the locomotive remained in its usual depot had obviously nothing to do with war reparations. The example shown here was incorporated into the Reichsbahn as 13 402 following the German invasion in 1939. (*Hermann Maey*)

Not a beauty yet: an S 4 with a superheater in the smokebox

This locomotive was delivered by Henschel in 1906 with the identity 52 *Erfurt*. The thick tubes on the smokebox show the early form of the smokebox-located superheater, before the fully developed superheater tubes followed in the smokebox. Incidentally, the Prussian State Railway numbered the saturated and superheated classes in different number series from 1906.

An overestimated superheated 4-4-0: the S 6

Robert Garbe's courage in developing the superheated locomotive soon turned into an overestimation of its potential. At a time when train weights throughout Europe needed six-coupled engines, he was still creating 4-4-0s as late as 1906. He alone of German locomotive engineers ventured to bear the weight of the locomotive on just four axles.

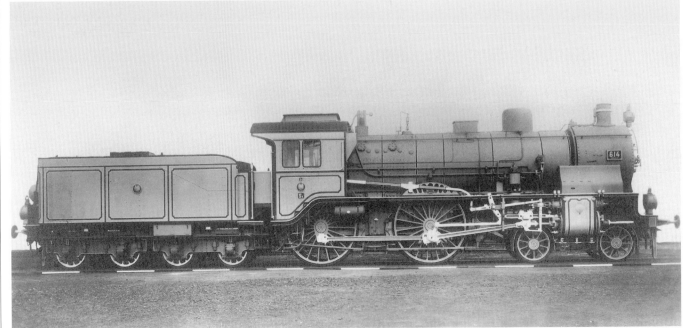

Large diameter wheeled 4-4-0s built	
Operator and manufacturer	**Number**
Those built for the north and west companies that were later in the KPEV nationalised railway by the Canada Works of the Schleswig Railway (1865 – 1866)	2
Prussian State Railway (KPEV) by BMAG, Borsig, Grafenstaden, Hanomag, Henschel, Humboldt, Schichau, Union and Vulcan (1890 – 1913)	2,285
Alsace-Lorraine Railway by BMAG, Borsig, Hanomag, Henschel, Grafenstaden, and Union, (1892 – 1913)	109
Royal Bavarian State Railway by Maffei (1892 – 1900)	139
Royal Württemberg State Railway by Esslingen (1854 – 1909)	133
Archduke's Baden State Railway by MBG Karlsruhe And Grafenstaden (1854 – 1900)	188
Royal Saxon Railway by Hartmann (1870 and 1891 – 1900)	60
Oldenburg State Railway by Hanomag (1903 – 1913)	17
Lübeck-Büchen Railway by BMAG and Linke-Hofmann (1907 – 1911)	7
In traffic up to about 1930	

The magic words: 'uniflow cylinders'
An S 6 with the number 657 *Halle* stands ready to depart from Berlin Anhalt station. The instruments above the cylinders are reminiscent of the unsuccessful attempts to separate the incoming and outgoing steam passages of the Stumpf Uniflow system.

Captured in Poland
In the end, the 584 examples of the S 6 must be considered as a failed investment: many of them barely lasted twenty years, and some only managed ten. With the invasion of Poland in 1939, units once again entered the German State Railway. Here, 13 530 is photographed in reasonable condition in 1941. (*Hermann Maey*)

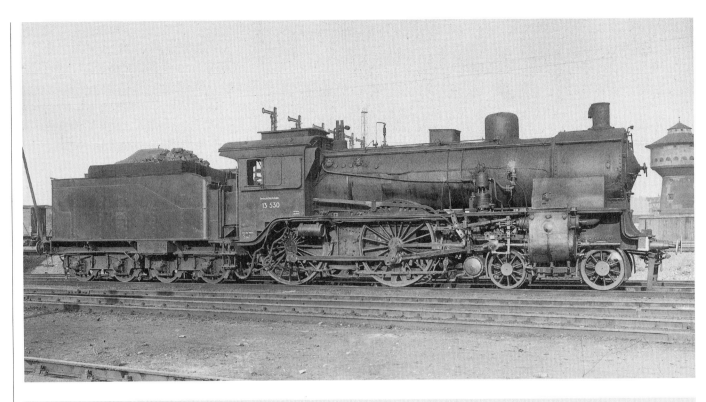

A 4-4-0 in Württemberg
While Bavaria, Baden and Saxony rightly turned their backs on the 4-4-0s in the twentieth century, between 1907 and 1909 the Württemberg Railway had their in-house works at Esslingen and built the last superheated express 4-4-0s in Germany. Unfortunately, it was too late for such modest constructions to be successful, and seen here is 13 1711 shortly before its withdrawal. (*Hermann Maey*)

2-4-2 Express locomotives

Before we leave the history of the 4-4-0s, we should also mention their less common competitors. Railways in France, Belgium, Württemberg and the Bavarian Palatinate were ordering and building 2-4-2 express locomotives, and even if they offered a strange and less than dynamic appearance with their compressed axle arrangement, they certainly proved their worth. Only in Italy did dainty large-wheeled 2-6-0s prove successful for decades on light expresses on level routes. A good riding experience could be achieved with just one pair of leading wheels when combined with a movable front axle to form a frame which, similar to a fixed bogie, took over the guidance when on a curved track. The best-known arrangement, especially in Germany, was the Krauss-Helmholtz bogie, named after the Munich manufacturer and its chief designer. Such bogie arrangements

The Palatinate Railway 2-4-2

A variation of the 4-4-0 was the 2-4-2. The Palatinate Railway had Krauss build twenty-two examples of their P 2 I between 1891 and 1896. The bringing together of the leading running wheels and the front coupled axle in the Krauss-Helmholtz arrangement guaranteed good riding quality and the rear trailing wheel axle left plenty of room for a large firebox and grate area. However, its performance for an express locomotive was modest. It could haul 180 tons at a steady 45mph through the forests of the Palatinate.

Built in Belgium
The 2-4-2 of the Main-Neckar Railway, built by the Belgian firm Cockerill, was more powerful than its Palatinate sister. After nationalisation in 1902, it became class S 2 of the Royal Prussian State Railway. The fifteen members of the class spent their last days in the Ruhr area and were withdrawn shortly after the First World War.

2-4-2 LOCOMOTIVES BUILT	
Operator and manufacturer	**Number**
Main-Neckar and Hesse-Ludwig Railways, later nationalised in the KPEV Railway by Cockerill and Krauss (1892 – 1902)	28
Palatinate Railway by Krauss (1891 – 1896)	22
In service until approximately 1923	

were the prerequisite for the success of five, six and seven axle express and local passenger locomotives with the 2-6-2, 2-6-4, 2-8-2 and 2-8-4 wheel arrangements throughout Europe.

The further development of the 4-4-0 went in two directions: for express locomotives, the almost forgotten rear trailing axle of the 2-4-2 lengthened the 4-4-0 to a 4-4-2 'Atlantic'. For modern slow passenger and mixed traffic work, as well as with some successful express locomotives, an extra coupled wheel was inserted between the bogie and the coupled axles forming a 4-6-0.

The Atlantic: the legendary 4-4-2

The 4-4-2 locomotives were named 'Atlantics' after the American precursor, although the first locomotive in the world with this wheel arrangement had been built in Austria in 1895. The first Atlantic in Germany appeared in 1898 on the Palatinate Railway, and the other regional states, apart from Württemberg, followed suit over the next decade.

The Atlantic offered the best layout for fitting a better and more efficient boiler: if the trailing axle

was not placed too closely to the rear coupled axle, there was room enough for a very large firebox and grate onto which a well proportioned long boiler could be attached, overhanging the front bogie. Often, however, the rear axle was used to support the increasing weight of a much larger locomotive, moving it nearer the rear coupled axle and therefore negating the potential of a significant increase in the size of the firebox complex. Real innovations in the valve gear and motion were utilised. Only a few 4-4-0s were fitted with four cylinders, but nearly all of the Atlantics were four-cylinder compound engines. Alfred de Glehn (1848 – 1936) was active at the Alsace Grafenstaden Engineering Works and his valve gear and motion were especially elegant. As

a result, locomotive developments in Germany and France were enriched by many innovations. His compound system worked with small outside high pressure cylinders between the bogie and the first coupled axle, and the large, low-pressure cylinders were inside above the bogie. The high-pressure cylinders drove the second axle and the low pressure cylinders the first coupled axle. Two of the most exotic locomotives belonging to the Atlantic group were also sent to Germany: the Bavarian State Railway was stimulated by the USA's own developmental work and ordered a truly innovative box of tricks, consisting of two 4-4-2s and a 2-8-0 from the leading manufacturer, Baldwin, as well as a few four-axle bogie coaches and a four-axle buffet car.

The first German Atlantic
The history of the 'Atlantic', technically the aforesaid 4-4-2, began in Germany with a remarkable construction. Between 1898 and 1904 the Palatinate Railway ordered twelve express locomotives from Krauss with two inner cylinders and a combination of external and internal frames. The *Saale* ran from 1898 to 1925.

Total rebuild
The P 3 I was found to be unsatisfactory and was therefore rebuilt in 1913 – 1914 as a four-cylinder compound machine. The existing inner cylinders now served as high-pressure cylinders, and new low-pressure cylinders were installed on the outside. After little more than a decade these eccentric locomotives had served their time. (*Stephan Beständig Collection*)

A booster axle

The Palatinate Railway continued to have a mind of its own. Its next P 3 II from 1900, like the Bavarian 4-2-2-2 pictured earlier, was fitted with a booster axle in between the wheels of the front bogie. The cylinders for the main coupled wheels lay inside. A special feature was the balancing of the mass of the motion through mobile counterweights under the firebox, but within a year, all these eccentricities had been set aside.

An X V in Dresden Altstadt (Old Town) depot

A beautiful shot of X V No.181 taken on 1 May 1923 in the Dresden Altstadt depot. It was withdrawn before receiving its DR number of 14 202. The bogie wheel brakes were not a regular feature at that time.

A Saxon Atlantic
The fifteen examples of the Saxon X V built between 1900 and 1903 were conventionally configured, saturated steam locomotives with four-cylinder compound propulsion, which were intended for express trains on the Berlin – Dresden route. No company and no manufacturer in Germany was prepared to reject this form of 'windcutter' cab at the turn of the century.

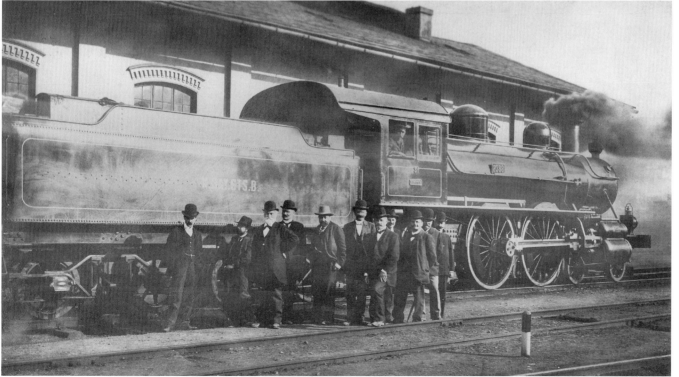

Two German express engines imported from the USA
Only once, after the pioneering days of the railroad industry, did a German company import locomotives from the USA. In 1901 Bavaria ordered two 4-4-2s and a 2-8-0 from Baldwin. The 4-4-2's valve gear and motion were unique, with one high-pressure and one low-pressure cylinder on each side of the locomotive, both located on the outside of the frame, as patented by Vauclain. One lasting innovation of the S 2/5 Vauclain engine was its bar frame.

Milestone: the Baden Railway IId

After looking at the collection of 4-4-0s and 2-4-2s and the earlier 4-4-2s, it is clear what an enormous leap the Baden State Railway and the Maffei Company took with their IId. The cylinder arrangements, the coupled wheels, the long boiler and firebox and grate between the rear coupled axle and trailing wheels demonstrated powerful ambition. The only shame is that a superheater was not included. On test journeys, the Atlantic touched 90mph.

The unusual construction (of the USA imports) confirmed the Royal Bavarian State Railway's decision to choose bar frames for all future high-performance locomotives.

These machines, which in many ways were surprisingly slipshod in their design details, had to be immediately reworked and adapted to German standards, but were still in service until 1923. Contrary to the usage made of the 2-2-2s, the 2-4-0s and the 4-4-0s, there was an entrenched opinion that the 4-4-2s, like the 4-2-0s previously, were

Building for the future
The IId was obviously intended for the Baden main line from Mannheim – Heidelberg – Karlsruhe – Basle, which has always been one of the fastest stretches of track in Germany.

exclusively for express passenger train work. As they were unable to offer any increased adhesion, the 4-4-2s were the runners of light trains on the flat, compared with the similar 4-6-0s. For this type of work, many Atlantics were given especially large driving wheels, thus enhancing their elegant effect. Many designs were outstanding

beauties, but the Atlantic's star waned faster in Germany than in France or Austria; its lack of adhesion limiting its potential usage. However, the fact the German 4-4-2s and the considerably older 4-4-0s were being withdrawn at the beginning of the 1920s was not only due to the limits of the design, but also because of the

peculiarity that virtually all variants continued to use saturated steam and were unable to compare with the 4-6-0s and 4-6-2s which had superheaters. This backwardness is particularly regrettable in the case of the otherwise excellent Prussian S 9 from 1908, which must have seemed obsolete even on its very first day of operation.

Elegant and capable
Technically, the P 4 from Maffei in 1905, now with wide firebox, was a further development of the S 2/5. This wonderful plate photograph allows us to see every detail of this elegant machine. (*Stephan Beständig Collection*)

Prussian S 7 of the Hanover type

After a row of remarkable southern German designs, we once again turn to Prussia. Many firms presented possible designs for an express locomotive, which, while fundamentally maintaining the dimensions of the existing 4-4-0s, now had the advantage of a longer boiler on the 4-4-2 layout. Hanomag's design was the S 7 of the 'Hanover' class, of which 159 were delivered between 1902 and 1906.

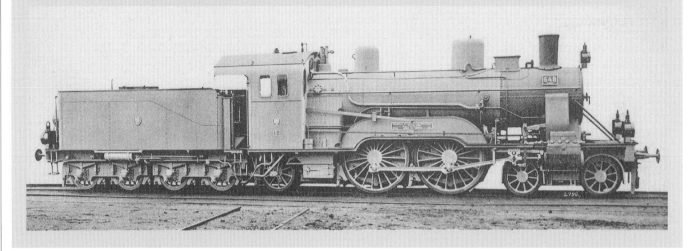

An express comes through Hamburg

We have already seen the S 3 in the busy street scene of Hamburg, and here we see an S 7 on the same curious journey. It will take the Hamburg – Cologne express as far as Osnabrück.

Already old-fashioned when new: the S 9
While Henschel was working on the numerous more up-to-date S 10 engines, Hanomag built ninety-nine saturated steam Atlantics from 1908, the first example of which is seen here. Perhaps if it had had a superheater it might have had a future, but they were scrapped, together with the 4-4-0s, in the 1920s.

The longest runs without engine change in the Prussian network in 1908

Route	Distance
Stendal – Dortmund	224 miles
Cologne – Kreiensen	191 miles
Hamburg (Altona) – Berlin	183 miles
Berlin – Saalfeld	183 miles
Königsberg – Bromberg	181 miles

The Alsace S 7
The engineering firm Grafenstaden from Mulhouse, in Alsace, which belonged to Germany between 1871 and 1918, carried on its own traditions. Its three variants of the S 7 were de Glehn's four-cylinder compounds with conspicuous high-pressure cylinders set further back. Some Prussian directorates combined together to produce seventy-nine examples between 1902 and 1905.

The beauty of the railway
This atmospheric winter shot of an S 7 with its clouds of smoke and steam is a rare treasure.

The only superheated Atlantics in Germany
The Saxon Railway Company was the only organisation in Germany to send a superheated Atlantic into service. Between 1909 and 1913, Hartmann built eighteen of the two-cylinder X H I engines. The boiler was similar to that of the XII H I, with a 4-6-0 wheel arrangement.

Key to the twentieth century: the construction workers
A peek into the Hartmann Works in Chemnitz. Photographed in 1913, the workers proudly present the ready to run X H I No.95, later 14 314 of the German State Railway. The skilled labourers shown here worked hand in hand with the engineers.

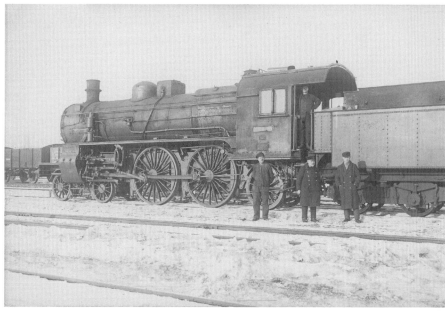

Portrait of a locomotive in the first winter of peace
The short-lived 14 308 of the German State Railway, formerly the Royal Saxon Company's No. 88, in a winter photograph taken in January 1919.

4-4-2s BUILT (ALL LARGE-WHEELED)	
Manufacturer	Number
KPEV by Henschel, Hanomag, Linke-Hofmann and Grafenstaden (1902 – 1910)	337
Royal Bavarian State Railway by Baldwin and Maffei (1901 and 1904)	12
Royal Saxon State Railway by Hartmann (1900 – 1903 & 1913)	33
Palatinate Railway by Krauss and Maffei	24
In service until around 1930	

The Wittfeld-Kuhn construction

We leave the large number of 4-4-2 classes and turn to the rarities with both a front and rear bogie. No deep explanation is needed as to why the supposedly streamlined three-cylinder compound 'removal van' built by Henschel in 1904 proved to be a failure.

Two rarities, one beauty: the 4-4-4

Proud announcements from the electrical industry caused panic elsewhere: the military railway south of Berlin had conducted trials with a three-phase electric unit, which had reached previously unheard of speeds. The Siemens vehicle had achieved 129.2mph on 23 October 1903 and an AEG unit 131.4mph on 28 October. No one had ever travelled that fast before and the locomotive construction industry no doubt feared for its future in the face of the electric traction vehicles' success. Both the popular and engineering media were already fully anticipating a bold Utopia of electrically hauled high-speed transport across the entire continent. Ideas of new tube and high-level railways had been abandoned, but were still enjoying life in the enthusiasts' imagination! There is nothing you can name that had not already been sketched out before the First World War. We've already seen how 1903 saw a late flowering of innovation and speed, and just two months after the record-breaking runs in Brandenburg, the Wright brothers made transport history by undertaking the first proven and documented flight in the world. Meanwhile, that same year, Henry Ford started making automobiles on his production line.

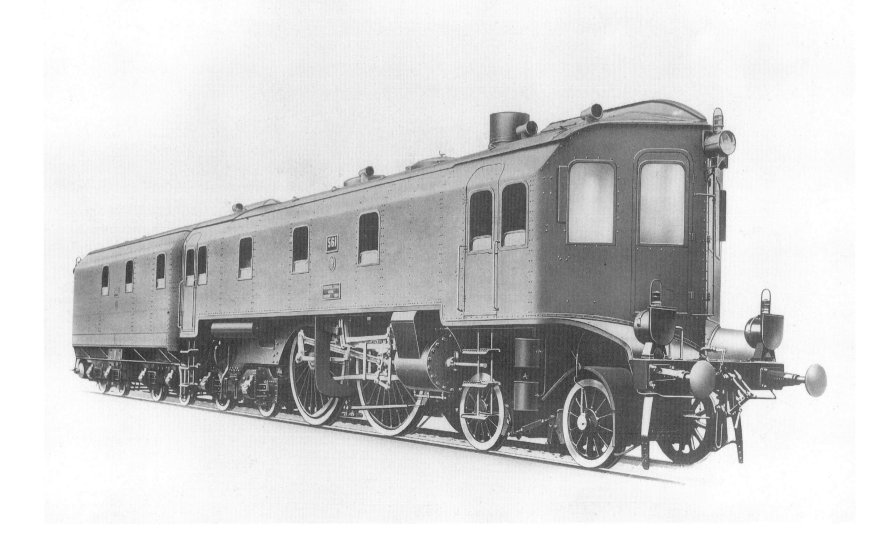

4-4-4s (ALL LARGE-WHEELED) BUILT	
Operator and manufacturer	Number
KPEV 1904 by Henschel	2
Royal Bavarian State Railway 1906 by Maffei (built on own Initiative later accepted by State Railway)	1

Conventional locomotive works were challenged to prove that their products could reach 150kph (94mph). In cooperation with the Royal Prussian State Railway (KPEV), in 1904 Henschel built two highly unusual high-speed locomotives with the 4-4-4 wheel arrangement. The names of Henschel's chief engineer and his opposite number at KPEV were commemorated in the class name 'Wittfeld-Kuhn'. The 7ft 2in coupled wheels with a three-cylinder compound system were highly ambitious, although it was known that the distribution of steam from a middle high-pressure cylinder to the two outside low-pressure cylinders was difficult to regulate. Unfortunately, locomotives' design was obsolete from the beginning due to the fact they did not include a superheater, which by that time was standard practice. Both machines were laughable curiosities thanks to their use of experimental streamlining and the footplate being placed at the front. The first of the two had the streamlining extended over the tender and had to put up with the nickname 'Removal Van'! For the second locomotive, the long boiler and tender were spared any streamlining. Today we know that the V-shaped edge at the front, intended to reduce wind pressure, had little aerodynamic advantage, and the working conditions for the driver in front of the smokebox were unreasonable (the fireman kept his place at the back, as usual).

Simply the most beautiful locomotive built
In complete breath-taking contrast to the Kuhn-Wittfeld vehicle mentioned previously, Maffei built one of the most beautiful German locomotives, the one-off S 2/6. Only the air pump beside the wide firebox disturbs the harmony of the whole picture. (*Hermann Maey*)

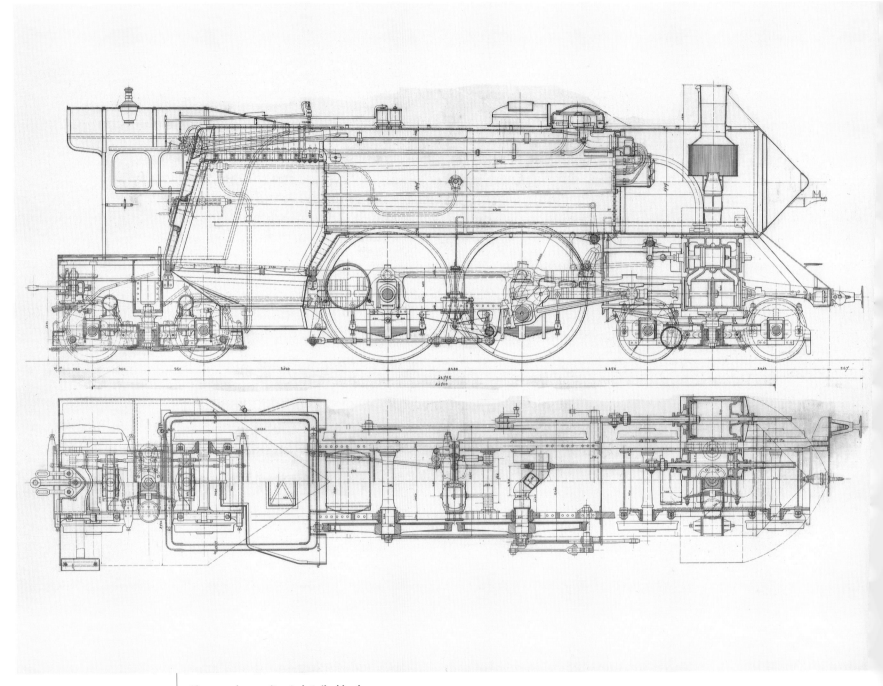

***Above and opposite*: A detailed look**
The display of the S 2/6 in a museum provides the opportunity to examine the drawings of both the inner and outer working parts of these locomotives. Recognisable here is the common pattern of firebox, long boiler, smokebox, cylinders, valve gear, motion and frames. Finding the ideal proportion for all of these parts was the goal of every engineer for over a century.

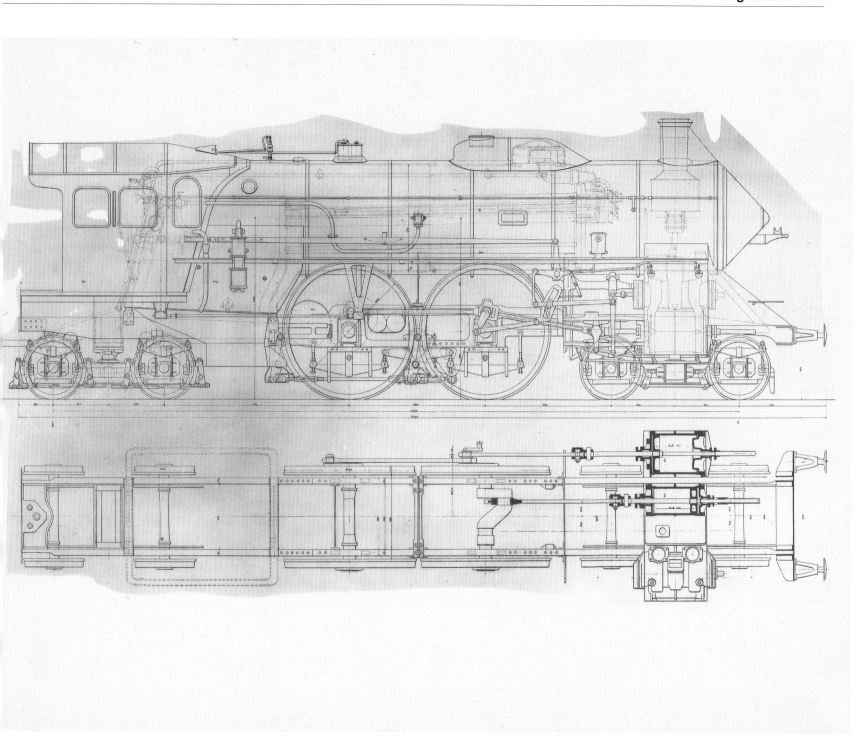

The Wittfeld-Kuhn engine fell far short of the required 90mph, managing just 80mph with a train of 221 tons. With 109 tons (less than the weight of engine and tender) it managed 85.6mph. The Munich manufacturer Maffei and its chief engineer Anton Hammel fared differently. In 1906 Maffei built a 4-4-0 with the intention of displaying it at a national exhibition. Corresponding to the principles that had become a matter of course in just a few short years, it was equipped with bar frames, a superheater, and the four-cylinder compound system. The resulting S 2/6 also had 7ft 2in coupled wheels. With a conventional structure, the high-speed locomotive was given a wind-smoothed appendage between the bufferbeam and smokebox, as well as a conical smokebox door and a windshield for the driver's cab. The result was one of the most beautiful locomotives ever built in Germany, which also managed to achieve the longed-for success: on 2 July 1907 it reached 154.5kph (96.56mph) on the route between Augsburg and Munich, setting the world record for steam locomotives.

In outline: the motion of the S 2/6
The S 2/6 preserved in the DB museum in Nuremberg. A glimpse of its moving parts provokes dreams of high-speed travel from more than 100 years ago. (*Andreas Knipping*)

Chapter 3

THE BASIC EUROPEAN PATTERN FOR THE TWENTIETH CENTURY

Three-coupled axles

Success with superheater: the 4-6-0

From around 1895, the six-coupled engine with front bogie was seen almost everywhere in Europe. To begin with it was mainly those railways with several steeply graded routes, such as in France, Baden, Bavaria and Austria, who hauled their expresses and stopping trains with 4-6-0 locomotives. Saturated steam engines with this wheel arrangement, conventional low-pitched boiler and four-cylinder compound systems, as in the Baden IV e of 1894 and an 1896 prototype and 1899 production of the Bavarian C V, remained only moderately successful in operation. The greater weight of the five-axle locomotive and its own resistance of the four-cylinder motion, plus the three-axle drive, sapped the reserve of the boiler, meaning the advantage over a 4-4-0 was reduced to simply a matter of greater adhesion.

The career of the 4-6-0 suddenly improved when the designers switched to a higher pitched boiler, bar frames, and, a little later, to the provision of superheaters. With the introduction of the Bavarian S 3/5 N in 1903 and the S 3/5 H a little later in 1908, the older C V locomotives were pushed into the background, while the even older 4-4-0s of the B XI class were silenced altogether. From 1910 onwards, the family of S 10 locomotives played an important role in the haulage of express trains in Prussia for the next forty years or so. Interestingly, the organisation had the choice between three variants:

- the S 10 as a four-cylinder superheated 4-6-0
- the S 10 1 as a four-cylinder superheated compound 4-6-0
- the S 10 2 as a three-cylinder superheated 4-6-0.

The four-cylinder compound machine, the S 10 1 (built in similar variations in 1911 and 1914) was the most successful, although both of the other classes performed very well in measured test conditions.

Bavaria's conservative 4-6-0
This 4-6-0 takes us back to the end of the nineteenth century. After taking over an example from 1896, the Royal Bavarian State Railway ordered forty-two more of the CV (1899 – 1901) from Maffei. The boiler reserve and adhesion was naturally greater than that of the 4-4-0 B XI, however the saturated four-cylinder compound engine fell below expectations.

S 3/5 on the German State Railway
Twenty examples of the saturated and twenty-four of the superheated versions of the S 3/5 came to the German State Railway. The 17 419 from 1907 is recognised as a harmonious, contemporary four-cylinder compound locomotive. Meanwhile, the Prussian Railway was still ordering old-fashioned 4-4-0s and 4-4-2s.

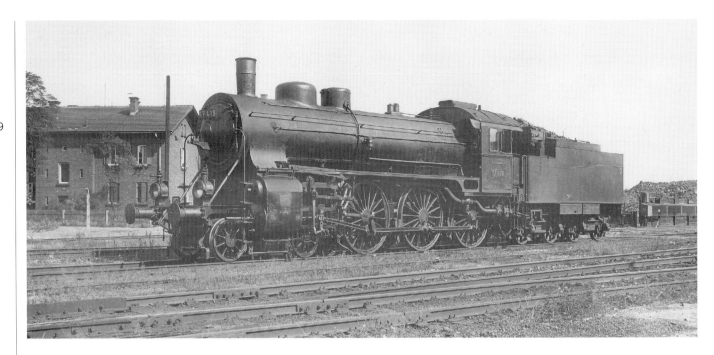

Saturated and superheated S 3/5
This French postcard is a reminder of the turning point for all of the regional state railways, namely the deliveries to the victorious powers following the armistice of 1918, which is wrongly described in various railway literature as being part of 'war reparations'. Twenty-five of the sixty-nine modern Bavarian 4-6-0s of the S 3/5 class found their way to Belgium and France. Here, 3357 has kept its Bavarian railway number on the French Eastern Railway.

The Saxon XII HV
The photographic collection on which a book like this is based does not simply appear from nowhere. So many photographs have been purchased, given as gifts or inherited over many years, and each has its own story. The first owner of this photograph of 17 755, a Saxon XII HV from 1914, has noted on the back that it was taken on 27 June 1931, shortly before the engine's withdrawal on 30 June 1932.

A 'simple' version
Compared with the compound XII HV built between 1906 and 1914, Saxony introduced a two-cylinder 'simple' version in 1909. However, one had to be content with only nine examples, which were divided between the French Eastern Railways and the German State Railway in 1918.

A well-engineered construction: the Prussian S 10

After a procession of Prussian express locomotives since the S 3, a maturity was finally reached in the 4-6-0 in 1910 and would last for decades to come. The three-coupled axles gave the S 10 the necessary adhesion and by simply increasing the distance of the first-coupled axle from the bogie, a four-cylinder drive was possible.

The S 10 as a Reichsbahn locomotive

This is an example of how the original S 10 looked during the Reichsbahn period. 17 002 was built by the firm BMAG in 1911 and withdrawn in 1933. The four-cylinder 4-6-0 remained controversial: the alleged excessive fuel consumption was hard to prove when compared with the other S 10 versions, and for long runs like Cologne – Altona (Hamburg) it achieved good results for two decades.

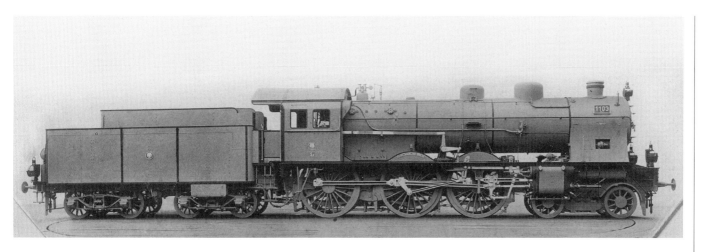

The Prussian S10.1
Parallel classes remained a Prussian speciality for optional procurement by the railway companies. The KPEV, in cooperation with Henschel, achieved the undisputed success of the century with the S 10.1. Using the de Glehn system, the 1911 version had its drive on the second main axle from the external high-pressure cylinders, and the internal low-pressure cylinders on the first-coupled axle.

A mature design
No. 1102 *Bromberg* received the number plate 17 1008 when it was absorbed into the German State Railway stock, along with smoke deflectors, a feedwater heater in front of the cab and a turbo-generator on the smokebox. The tail-rod covers of the inner valve gear protrude over the bufferbeam. It was withdrawn from the Western Zone of the State Railway in 1949. (*Carl Bellingrodt*)

An S 10.1 in the centre of Berlin

The S 10.1 made a name for itself in the great cities during the times of the Kaiser, the Weimar Republic and the swastika, as well as in the loneliness of long-distance journeys. Here it stands on the main line of the Berlin-Alexanderplatz station, facing east.

An S 10.1 of the 1914 series

Judged equal in rank to the 1911 series was the 1914 class. The eye is easily deceived, and one suspects with the higher pitch of the boiler that at exactly 9ft 6in, its height is the same as the coupled wheel diameter of 6ft 5in. The four cylinders are, however, arranged in a single horizontal block.

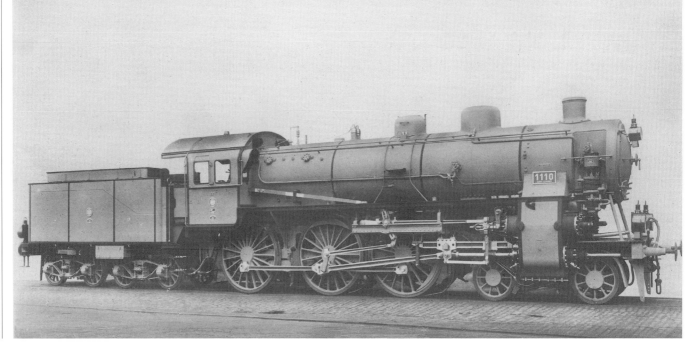

The fact that the unassuming two-cylinder superheated 4-6-0 in the shape of the Prussian P 8 should become the classic German (as well as the Polish, Romanian and Belgian) mixed traffic and stopping passenger locomotive must be mentioned here, because with its resilient boiler and maximum speed of 100kph (62mph), it also performed well in express train service. Indeed, the uninterrupted use of 4-6-0 locomotives in Germany, which lasted some eighty years after 1894, is thanks to the P 8. It also acted as the gravedigger for all the 4-4-0s and 4-4-2s in the early 1920s. Whilst these latter examples rarely reached more than 70 or 75mph in traffic, the six-coupled P 8 sailed ahead with its good acceleration from a stationary position and its excellent and steady performance on adverse gradients.

The comfortable placing of the firebox and ashpan between the coupled axles for the 4-4-0s was no longer possible. Both rear axles were moved further apart and the original square grate was lengthened and the firebox extended forward. The proverbial long narrow firebox thus emerged and was to become the trademark of many Prussian, as well as French, locomotives of many different wheel arrangements, producing efficient steam performance in the hands of experienced firemen.

LARGE-DIAMETER WHEELED 4-6-0s	
Operator and manufacturer	**Number**
KPEV by BMAG, Hanomag, Henschel, Linke-Hofmann and Vulcan (1910 – 1916)	563
Royal Bavarian State Railway by Maffei (1899 – 1911)	111
Royal Saxon State Railway by Hartmann (1906 – 1912)	55
Alsace-Lorraine State Railway by Grafenstaden and Henschel (1902 – 1915)	127
Lübeck-Büchen Railway by Henschel	15
In traffic until 1961	

On the Reichsbahn
The S10 I class of 1914 now makes an appearance in the Reichsbahn era. We can see here that 17 1137 is a functional as well as a handsome machine. Once again we must emphasize that the Prussian administration immediately replaced the overtaxed four-coupled S5 2, S6 and S7 with such locomotives. (*Carl Bellingrodt*)

Built in the First World War

In practice, the S10 2 was assessed against the aforementioned classes (the S10 and S10 I) and thus proved that the class could perform well with several boiler and motion variations, provided the right dimensions were chosen and the details carefully executed. The Vulcan 3000/1915 ran on the Reichsbahn as 17 233.

With the State Railway

Now renamed 17 254, the former 1213 *Münster* joined the huge locomotive fleet of the German State Railway. Nearly all the S10 2 (17 2) locomotives were in service in the western regions of Prussia and Germany, and were withdrawn not long after the Second World War. (*Carl Bellingrodt*)

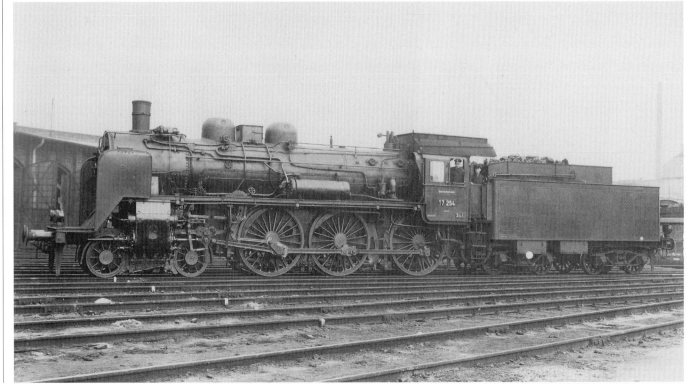

High-pressure locomotive
The S10 2 was the only former regional state railway class that was tested with a high-pressure boiler. 17 206 was rebuilt in 1925 as a high-pressure compound locomotive, renamed as H 17 206, made an unusual impression with its 870lbs psi two-chamber boiler.

Middle-pressure locomotive
On the other hand, 17 236 and 17 239 were rebuilt in 1932 with an inconspicuous 365lbs psi medium-pressure boiler. In this case the compound machines operated the internal cylinder using high-pressure and the external cylinders with low-pressure. In reality, the correct application of the high pressure was not practicable in daily running because of the quality of the steel needed. (*Carl Bellingrodt*)

The Oldenburg S10

We must not leave the 4-6-0 without reference to a particularly hapless competitor, the German 2-6-2, a six-coupled engine with a Krauss-Helmholtz front truck and a rear axle. Such locomotives were successful in large numbers in Austria, Italy, Yugoslavia, Czechoslovakia, Great Britain and the Soviet Union, yet just three examples were built for the Oldenburg Railway, and they really never paid for themselves. The simple P8 exceeded it by far in performance, speed, fuel economy and repair costs. Even more radical was France's complete abandonment of tender locomotives with this wheel arrangement. Only after 1945 was the 2-6-2 wheel arrangement rehabilitated in both parts of Germany, namely as a local and stopping passenger engine with the ability to give a lively performance on express trains.

Hanomag's failed attempt for Oldenburg
Innovative ideas led to the consideration of the single German 2-6-2 express class and also the only one with Lentz valve gear. Unfortunately, success was unforthcoming.

LARGE DIAMETER WHEELED 2-6-2s	
Manufacturer	Number
Oldenburg State Railway by Hanomag (1917)	3

The Pacific wins

After knowing what to do about the lack of adhesion with the 4-4-2 and the limits of the narrow firebox, the next step in development should come as no surprise: the basic layout of the 4-6-0 was supplemented by the trailing axle of the 4-4-2. A really high-performance boiler could be supported by six axles and the adhesion of the six-coupled wheels left nothing to be desired for express train services. Just a few months after the French saturated steam prototype with conventional frames appeared, Maffei followed suit with the Baden IV f; the first German Pacific. It was fashioned according to the modern concept with a superheater, bar frames and wide firebox. Unfortunately, a compromise had been made between the needs for the level Rhine Valley stretch and the steep Black Forest route, thus resulting in a driving wheel diameter of just 5ft 11in. Consequently, the IV f was not fast enough on the level ground and not powerful enough on the inclines. The Pacific was soon victorious on practically all the main lines in France and Germany (except Prussia). On the various German regional state railways, all the Pacifics were superheated and, apart from the Saxon XV III H, were four-cylinder compounds. Only the Alsace-Lorraine Railway built the 'de Glehn' type. Baden, Bavaria, Württemberg and Saxony chose – with the exception of the Baden IV h – the 'von Borries' system, where the four cylinders and steamchests were level over the front bogie and under the smokebox, and all four sets of motion drove the middle axle.

From Munich for Baden
It made sense to combine the three-coupled axles of the 4-6-0 with the large back section of the 4-4-2 to form the 4-6-2. The Baden State Railway wanted a type that could operate on the flat Rhine Valley as well as on the steep Black Forest route. The IV f built by Maffei in 1907 was unable to meet both of these requirements.

A legend is born
Using the basic construction of the IV f, with 6ft diameter wheels instead of 5ft 11in, Maffei created the Bavarian S3/6, which today is considered to have been one of the most successful express locomotives in Germany. Theorists and operators are of the same opinion that its success was not based on any particular piece of ingenuity, but on an ideal balancing of firebox, long boiler, compound system, motion and valve gear. We see here the second example, 3602, which has been specially prepared and decorated for the 1908 Munich Exhibition.

With 925 engines, Germany was second only to France in terms of numbers of Pacifics (France had approximately 1,350). From around 1930 to 1960, and therefore after the significant reduction of the 4-6-0s due to the noticeable advance of diesel and electric motive power, the Pacific was by far the dominant locomotive for express trains in Germany. Of particular note were:

- The splendid series of four-cylinder compound machines from Maffei, from the Baden IV f to the legendary Bavarian S3/6, of which 159 examples were built in different variations over twenty-two years. It remained the best German express locomotive for undulating routes and for speeds of between 50 and 75mph. Their finale came at the end of the First World War, along with the end of the regional state railways, with

A real beauty
After the images of countless former regional state railway classes that had been withdrawn earlier, the era of the Reichsbahn can be seen here in the Prussian S10 family. The 18 442 represents the particularly elegant variant of the S3/6, with 6ft 6in instead of 6ft driving wheels. In operation, however, the 'high-wheelers' were not fundamentally superior to the standard version. (*Carl Bellingrodt*)

the Baden IV h, in which all the errors with the IV f were remedied. It remained the fastest German steam locomotive until 1935.

• Just as original and successful was the Alsace Lorraine S 12, with its trailing axle tucked behind the rear-coupled axle and narrow firebox, as was the elegant Württemberg class C and the Saxon XVIII H.

On the Prussian network, the S 10 family sufficed for the vast flatlands of northern Germany. Bearing in mind how quickly the 2-4-0, 4-4-0, 4-4-2 and 4-6-0 fell behind the demand of the operator – not to mention the demands of the politicians and media for ever faster trains – the immediate step up to the Pacific was inevitable. Despite this, they were not superseded until the end of the steam era.

The reasons behind the pause in construction of 4-6-2s can be found in history in general. The outbreak of the First World War in 1914 interrupted the great period of express trains and peaceful competition that existed for the fastest trains. The first priority throughout Europe for railways now was to transport troops, the wounded, prisoners of war, and supplies, as well as raw materials for the enormous expansion of the armaments industry. It is also important to recognise that the express locomotive had reached a level of maturity that made further increases in performance non-urgent and thus further improvements were difficult. The Prussian S 10 I for north Germany and the Bavarian S 3/6 for the south were ideal locomotives for the haulage of typical expresses of the time; trains of ten or so coaches in the speed corridor of 55 – 75mph, constricted by the track occupation, signalling systems, the rolling stock types and braking systems available at the time.

S3/6 from Kassel
It was not until 1930 that Henschel built 18 537, making it one of the last steam locomotives constructed based on the original regional design. It remained a lasting compliment for Maffei and Bavaria and a bitter pill for the fathers of the new standard locomotives: even the 1930-built 03 showed no significant advantage over the S3/6's design, which was two decades older. (*Carl Bellingrodt*)

Unsurpassed even in the Weimar Republic
Ordered after the First World War and built in 1924, 18 509 is seen here a long way away from Bavaria in Rüdersheim alongside the Rhine – rather lacking in water – in full flight with D404 from Krefeld to Vienna. (*Carl Bellingrodt*)

The only Pacific in Württemberg

A well-proportioned and aesthetically successful Pacific for hilly terrain was the Württemberg C; the only modern express locomotive of that regional railway. The 'apron' below the running plate was unique. (*Carl Bellingrodt*)

A Württemberg engine in the Federal Railway (DB)

The C (later class 18 1) was in operation until 1955. This photograph of 18 118 was taken at this time, during the age of the federal railway. (*Carl Bellingrodt*)

S 12 from Alsace-Lorraine

In comparison with the Bavarian S3/6 the year younger Alsace-Lorraine S 12, a typical de Glehn compound, was scarcely a genuine Pacific but an earlier 4-6-0 with an additional supporting axle.

Built in the First World War

In the middle of the First World War the Saxon State Railway added another Pacific for expresses on the Dresden – Berlin route. The XVIII H was the first three-cylinder Pacific.

On the State Railway
The DR (East German Railway) continued to use the 18.0 in its Saxon stamping ground until the 1960s. (*Gerhard Illner*)

City atmosphere
A 'master shot' from the interwar period shows a current 18.0 in old Berlin crossing the Landwehr Canal on the Anhalt – Dresden line and under the high-level railway. The inscription at the bottom of the image reads, 'Berlin: The crossing of the high-level railway over the Anhalt Railway and Landwehr Canal.'

4-6-2s built for the State Railways (all large-wheeled)

We should also consider the 4-6-2s, but only in the time of the former state railways, including those built to the old regional designs in the Reichsbahn era.

Operator and manufacturer	Number
Archduke's Baden State Railway by Maffei (1907 – 1912, & 1918 – 1920)	55
Royal Bavarian Railway and German State Railway, by Maffei & Henschel (1908 -1918, 1923 – 1930)	149
Württemberg State Railway, by Esslingen (1913 – 1921)	41
Palatinate Railway by Maffei (1914)	10
Royal Saxon State Railway, by Hartmann (1917)	10
Grafenstaden (1909)	8
In service until 1965	

Record holder

The last regional state railway Pacific came just at the onset of the German State (Reichsbahn) Railway. The Baden IV h was the fastest German locomotive in 1918 and retained its position until 1935. The cylinder blocks for both high- and low-pressure cylinders were unusual. The reason for this was the transition to the drive on the second coupled axle, with the resulting moving forward of the inner cylinders. To relieve the strain on the middle-coupled axle, Maffei's Anton Hammel activated the internal motion on the front-coupled axle, meaning it now had only one crank axle.

The Adriatic 2-6-4

Before leaving the Pacifics, an important deviation should also be considered: the great locomotive engineer, Karl Gölsdorf, who was responsible for all locomotive classes of the Imperial Royal Austrian State Railway in the western half of the Danube monarchy's empire during the last twenty-five years of its existence,

'turning' the 4-6-2 into a 2-6-4. For reasons that remain unknown, the Prussian State Railway decided to purchase seven examples with watertube fireboxes and in 1919 identified them as class S 11. They were then sold to the Polish State Railway as early as 1921, although it already possessed a larger number of both Austrian 210 and 310 designs.

Large-wheeled 2-6-4 locomotives	
Operator and manufacturer	**Number**
Prussian State Railway by Florisdorf (1919)	7

In the service of the German State Railway
The smoke deflectors which were added later strengthened the impression of power of the German State Railway's Baden IV h or 18.3. The piston tail-rod covers from the internal cylinders jut out from the skirt behind the bufferbeam at rather odd angles. (*Carl Bellingrodt*)

Chapter 4

EXPRESS LOCOMOTIVES FOR THE REPUBLIC AND DICTATORSHIP

Larger than the 4-6-2: the heavy four-coupler

In 1918 the railways in a politically and economically shattered Europe had more things to worry about than the development of luxury long-distance trains. A short recovery was followed by the Great Depression and the resulting decline in traffic. When political and travel conditions were favourable once again in the 1930s, thoughts could return to longer and faster trains. However, other branches of railway technology had moved on from their 1914 positions. Lightweight all-welded carriages became more common and made further advancements in locomotive size less necessary. After the strengthening of the infrastructure of many main lines – which allowed an increase in axle weight from 14 – 15 tons to 18 – 20 tons – more power could be installed in six-axle engines than ever before. Many routes throughout Europe, which had at one time seen steam locomotives pushed to their limits, were now electrified. And wherever an acceleration of speedier business

travel was required in anticipation of investment programmes for track, signals, locomotives and carriages, diesel units were recommended.

A little later, the Second World War once more saw an extreme increase in transport volume within the framework of reduced timetables, which were geared to the timings of goods trains. Then followed years in which you were happy if the wheels turned at all, before finally, the whole era of complete electrification and dieselisation, with modern steam locomotives left to fight a rear-guard action

However, the enlargement of steam locomotives to more than six axles encountered several problems. If you wanted to improve the reserve of steam production and use a larger boiler with increased grate area, you could opt for a 4-6-4 wheel arrangement. Yet because the weight of such a machine could not be fully utilised for adhesion, the number of German, British, French, and Hungarian test versions of this wheel arrangement remained

small. More plausible was the use of four-coupled axles with the indubitable advantage of greater adhesion weight: a 2-8-2 need not be larger than a 4-6-2. However, it is precisely the increase of the coupled axles from three to four that disproportionately increases the resistance, indeed much more so than the move from two to three coupled axles. At the same time, a four-axled large wheel diameter engine with strengthened motion through the coupling rods is particularly awkward on curved track, points and crossings. To accelerate a machine with such a wheel arrangement with three or four sets of motion and maintain a constant speed of 60 – 75mph on the level, or 45 – 55 mph on long rising gradients, and also gain a noticeable improvement in performance at the drawbar, the boiler required could hardly be accommodated on fewer than seven load-bearing axles. A 2-8-4 or 4-8-2 would indeed be a true giant, throwing up more problems for movement onto turntables and shed lines.

The balance of such locomotives was often unsatisfactory: a seven- or eight-axle locomotive needed just as much coal for its own movement as it did to haul a train. It was also difficult to develop a suitable steam generator. Under European clearance limits, the boiler could only be enlarged lengthways, which had already met with its ideal proportions on the Pacific. In these circumstances, it is not surprising that the number of such express steam locomotives remained low when compared with the number of Pacifics. At the end of the regional state railway period there was only one genuine eight-coupled express steam locomotive type, namely the Saxon XX HV with 6ft 3in diameter driving wheels. As the largest, strongest and last state railway express steam locomotive, it aroused great admiration in 1918 when it appeared on the steeply graded Hof-Reichenbach-Chemnitz-Dresden- Görlitz route.

Yet the company was not entirely happy with the locomotive giant. In hindsight, because of the need to restrict its length in order to fit turntables, the inner cylinder motion of the four-cylinder machine was too compressed. Therefore, the steam passages to the high-pressure cylinders and between the high- and low-pressure cylinders were

The railway enthusiast's dream
This photograph, taken in 1935, shows the extremely well-maintained 39 126, 01 110 and 03 104 in the Hamm depot. Large smoke deflectors were a well-known international trademark of the Reichsbahn. (*Carl Bellingrodt*)

The Hartmann anniversary
The mighty Saxon XX HV was the only eight-coupled express locomotive of the old regional state railways. This postcard illustrates the distance travelled over sixty years from the ancient Via, which we recognise above. The text in the image reads, 'Engineering Factory of Rich. Hartmann Ltd of Chemnitz. The Jubilee locomotive 4,000 built for the Royal Saxon State Railway, 1918.'

too narrow, resulting in a critical loss of performance, and even experienced crews found it hard to accelerate to more than 55mph.

For the most part, the further development of the express steam locomotive beyond the Pacific took place overseas. The mighty class 114/214 of the Austrian national railway, which was built in 1927 with 6ft 4in diameter wheels, was able to reach speeds of 70 – 75mph. The 214 class was also seen on the railways of Romania, where the development of Russian or Soviet locomotives was hardly noticeable. For example, who knows about the impressive 649 examples of the 2-8-4 express steam locomotive of class NC (IS) with 6ft coupled driving wheels, built between 1932 and 1942? Although its class identity initials were for that of the cruel dictator, Joseph Stalin, it certainly did not reduce the performance of these designs.

The mighty XX HV
Observers waiting at platforms or level crossings had never seen such huge cylinders, such a rank of driving wheels, or such a long boiler before. It is always worth remembering that just a decade before the Saxon XX HV, the German standard was a 4-4-0, which was barely half as heavy.

Built during the First World War but still used in the German Democratic Republic
The influences of the Reichsbahn era are becoming increasingly clear in our gallery of images. The only noteworthy eight-coupled express locomotive in German railway history ran as class 19.0 and would see many eventful decades during its lifetime. (*Werner Hubert*)

Large-wheeled 2-8-2s	
Operator and manufacturer	**Number**
Saxon State Railway by Hartmann (1918 – 1923)	23
In operation until 1971	

The reliable one
It was not by chance that this P8 has a typical Prussian express train coupled up. For years Germany's insane policies created and maintained that reliable journeys with long trains running at 45 – 60mph were more important than any express journey. An ideal task for the thrifty and efficient Prussian.

The Prussian P10
In the sphere of the eight-coupled it was not the Saxon XX HV that won through, but the more modestly dimensioned three-cylinder P10 with the same wheel arrangement. There was a good balance between its major employment as a mixed traffic engine suitable for slow stopping passenger services and its success in running express trains. (*Carl Bellingrodt*)

The most important foreign 2-8-2 from a German point of view was the Polish Pt31, with its class identification denoting its year of construction: 1931. It was a surprisingly simple two-cylinder express engine with 6ft 1in diameter driving wheels for heavily graded routes. Conforming with the basic principles of the German State Railway standard locomotives, with near enough the same boiler proportions as the 01, it was odd that the latter's problems never really surfaced for the Pt31. Renumbered as class 19.1, the Pt31 met the requirements of German timetables and routes after they were looted in considerable numbers to Bavaria and the annexed Austria following the invasion of Poland. After the Second World War, the successful 2-8-2 was rebuilt in more modern form in Poland as class Pt47.

The 'nearly' express locomotive: the class 39

The moderate success of the large Saxon 2-8-2 did not mean that engines of this wheel arrangement had no role to play for express train working in Germany, even if its driving wheel diameter was below the limit considered appropriate for express working. The three-cylinder 39 from 1922 was ordered for express train working and was developed as the Prussian P10. With driving wheels of only 5ft 9in, this 2-8-2 was authorised for speeds of 70mph and classified as a mixed traffic locomotive, although it was used almost exclusively for express work in the more mountainous parts of the country. Early on, the 'Prussian' made its home in Baden, Württemberg, northern Bavaria

and Saxony, and its acceleration from stations with heavy trains, along with its steady persistence on gradients, was greatly valued. The handling of the 39 was not easy; like its French predecessors, the location of the grate and ashpan was over the rear axle, with the firebox spread out further forward, forcing it between the two rear-coupled axles. The fireman had to be experienced with the engine and be master of his trade in order to deliver sufficient coal to the far corners of the grate.

As a result, in the years following the amalgamation of the regional state railways in 1920 there was a radical reduction in the driving wheel diameter of locomotives considered appropriate for express work, to just 5ft 9in. The excellent

performance and economy of the 4-6-0 P8 (later to be class 38.10 of the German State Railway) has already been mentioned. By 1923 the number of these proud engines had risen to 3,438, a total far above the total number of available express locomotives and other mixed traffic and passenger engines. They could haul many fast and semi-fast services without any problems, while the 260 eight-coupled class 39s could cope with the heavier trains and those running on the more steeply graded routes. All the interesting 4-4-0s and 4-4-2s seen on the previous pages dating from the two decades before the First World War hardly played any role by the end of the conflict and were often scrapped after little more than ten years in operation.

Made for overseas
Locomotives were important export items, and German manufacturers built locomotives for countries such as Russia, France, Denmark, Norway, Italy, Spain, Yugoslavia, Hungary and Bulgaria. Here we see a Maffei Pacific built in 1922 during its transportation to Romania.

Sweaty work
A locomotive works during the change from the state era to the Reichsbahn, where a young man is forging a coupling rod. The manufacture of steam locomotives required tremendous hard work in the rolling mill, foundry and forge.

Locomotives for the Weimar Republic

The railway enthusiast has often read that the German State Railway (Deutsche Reichsbahn) was founded on 1 April 1920, but this description does not do justice to the historical context. The German Empire had lost the war and the 1918 armistice had led to an unbelievable compulsory blood letting of former regional state railway locomotives and carriages (often misleadingly considered as war reparations). This 'November revolution' had created a republic out of the former states and empire. In bitter and often armed struggles, parliamentary democracy, based on an only moderately modernised social order and supported by many of the elite, prevailed against the alternatives of revolutionary socialism or a nationalist dictatorship. In terms of foreign policy, an isolated Germany faced extreme war reparation demands from the victorious powers. As for domestic politics, millions of former soldiers needed work and homes, and hundreds of thousands of war-wounded and war widows needed state support. Violence in obscure theory as well as in bloody practice oppressed and threatened the young Weimar Republic from day one. In despairing defence, real patriots from different political backgrounds recognised the imperative for national responsibility. Matthias Erzberger, almost forgotten today, had been a representative of the Catholic Centre in parliament since 1903, and was also the head of the German delegation at the armistice negotiations in 1918. Among other

things, he had introduced a uniform income tax law, as well as taking charge of the takeover of the state railways and its administration. He was also responsible for the government's admittedly daring financial policy, which aimed to increase purchasing power and investment activity by increasing the volume of money available and thus accepting a state of constant inflation. However, he was not to witness the hyperinflation of

1923. The nationalist enemies of democracy had not forgotten Erzberger's involvement in the peace negotiations, and he was assassinated on 26 August 1921.

When the federal states handed over their railway assets to the German State Railway on 1 April 1920, they had been badly affected by the war and were in desperate need of attention. With the additional loss of those locomotives handed over for 'war

A portrait of the first 01
The Reichsbahn wanted to start a new era of locomotive construction and train promotion. A lack of basic concepts and unfavourable circumstances hindered complete success, but the 01.001 was impressive.

A railway enthusiast's dream
This 01 was still seen in the log post-war decades, albeit no longer with the glossy paintwork of the brand new 01.110.

reparations', the German State Railway found itself in possession of around 800 express 4-6-0s and 172 Pacifics. Among the latter, after deducting those given away as 'war reparations' were – according to a census of March 1920 – 55 Baden, 70 Bavarian, 37 Württemberg and 10 Saxon locomotives. There were then a further 70 examples of the Bavarian S 3/6 built up until

1930. The P8 and P10 replicas could be purchased relatively cheaply with the inflation money, while the railway committees and manufacturers drew up designs for the future.

At the same time as these locomotives were grouped as classes 17, 18 and 39 of the German State Railway, the first new 4-6-2s were built; the standard locomotives of classes 01 and 02.

The standard Pacifics 01 and 02 of the German State Railway

The committees of the German State Railway, which was reconstituted as the private German Railway Company (DRG) in 1924, felt obliged to adopt a rational and scientific way of thinking. In the locomotive construction industry, huge work was undertaken to standardise all parts subject to wear and tear with the goal of being able to exchange common parts between different classes during major works overhauls. The length of time spent in the repair shops, which were now economically structured, was soon able to be reduced from months to weeks. Consequently, locomotive availability grew so rapidly that the older classes could be withdrawn in large numbers. For new builds, as many parts and assemblies as possible were used that were common to different classes. Accordingly, the

development of the tried and tested regional state railways was out of the question, which meant the time of ongoing freedom and fruitful competition between manufacturers and railway administrations was over. What is more, the strict head of the Locomotive Department, Richard Paul Wagner (1882 – 1953) unceremoniously rejected all compound systems and all multi-cylinder varieties as 'playthings of the past'.

At the same time, he explained that the current state of steam locomotive development had reached the stage of final perfection – a statement that is always going to be problematic in the history of technology, as it is in so many other areas of human endeavour. Unfortunately, Wagner brought the locomotive subject committee and the headquarters of the State Railway to agree to his way of thinking for a decade and a half.

The class 02: doomed to fail
The 02 003 enters our photo gallery as the well-intentioned but out of place four-cylinder compound variety of the standard express locomotive. The ten examples were later rebuilt as 01s.

The stepchild of the Reichsbahn
Externally, the four-cylinder compound 02 006 can only be distinguished from an 01 by the protruding pistons under the smokebox door. (*Carl Bellingrodt*)

According to his specifications, the basic standard for a heavy main line locomotive was a heavy six-axle engine. Two types of motion were built for both express and goods engines. The 4-6-2 emerged as a two-cylinder engine (01) and four-cylinder compound (02), the showpiece of locomotive history, the goods engine as a two-cylinder machine (43), also with three cylinders (44). With ten examples of each, a fundamental scientific

and final comparison on both performance and economy should be successful. Admittedly, there were doubts about the outcome from the start. A design in the southern construction tradition with the signature of the leading Maffei company was not accepted.

The 02 received the different driving motion from the 01 without any other original additions. The steam chests and valves for the low-pressure cylinders were

demonstrably too small, meaning the machine was therefore working against a resistance that reduced its performance. Maffei offered to rebuild it, but Wagner was completely satisfied with the failure of the compound locomotive, having preferred a two-cylinder machine from the beginning.

With Wagner's critical words holding sway, nothing further was attempted beyond the capable superheated two-cylinder steam engine with the use of strong load-bearing bar frames. This construction style stemmed from modern American practice, where compounding and multi-cylindered locomotives had never taken hold. This resulted in cheaper construction and reduced repair costs, as there was no need for the crew to perform acrobatics to oil the inner motion. It must not be forgotten that many excellent former regional state railway designs were born out of time-related needs for strict axle weight or length limitations, as well as past concerns about weights on frames and motion. The 01 was undoubtedly an outstanding locomotive, even if, to meet speed and train weight requirements, it had to be pushed to the limit of its steam production and riding quality. The class was updated – to little economic value – by the lengthening of the boiler tubes from 19ft to 22ft at the cost of the length of the smokebox and by increasing the diameter of the bogie wheels from 2ft 9in to 3ft 3in, raising the maximum authorised speed from 75 to 81mph. The tender of the later builds was enlarged from 7,000 to 7,500 gallons capacity, although routes with short turntables at the destination points still required engines with the old small tenders. For example, stations at the border with the Netherlands used the old small tenders right up until the 1960s.

Their characteristic style, with the mighty boiler, huge flat smoke deflectors, the sloping cab sides and premier class number, made the 01 one of the most popular German locomotives, and what is more, one of the best-known products of our industrial age.

01 in the cross-border traffic between the two Germanys
The 01s typically hauled expresses between East and West Germany. Here 01 226 of Erfurt is leaving Bebra station in 1958 with a huge plume of smoke, taking the D 199 from Frankfurt-am-Main to Leipzig. The DDR's brown coal produced a great deal of smoke, but the depots of the German Federal Railway (DB) provided their East German colleagues with some hard coal during the turnround at the border. (*Carl Bellingrodt*)

Rare innovation: the five experimental Pacifics

The emergence of three completely different experimental Pacific designs was not due to the limited innovations of the Reichsbahn committees, but the struggle of the manufacturers who were under pressure from the early signs of the unstoppable advance of the electric and diesel locomotive industries. In 1924 Krupp presented the first German turbine locomotive at the Railway Technology Exhibition in Seddin, near Berlin. Instead of the conventional piston valve machine, it had a double turbine under the smokebox of the Zoelly system, with gears on a lower pinion, and from there onto the coupled three driving wheels. The obligation to fix large wheels to limit the speed of the pistons was obviously unnecessary in this case, and a wheel diameter of 5ft 5in sufficed. After many adjustments and alterations, it was finally possible to demonstrate a significant saving in coal when compared to the standard design. However, a disproportionately large amount of steam was used by the second turbine to generate backwards movement and guarantee drawing sufficient draught. The locomotive was incorporated into the Reichsbahn fleet as T 18 1001 and worked out of Hamm depot until 1939, together with the 01.

Maffei also tried its hand at a turbine locomotive, delivering one in 1926 with the Curtis turbine system. Like the Krupp engine, its use and performance of the drive mechanism matched initial hopes. But here, too, the complicated equipment for maintaining the feedwater system with the complex condensing gear consumed a great deal steam and, therefore, energy. This fact, as well as the high maintenance costs, drained away any theoretical achievable advantage of the turbine locomotive when compared with a piston valve engine. Apart from long periods in the works, the T 18 1002 remained active in express traffic in Bavaria until the Second World War.

At the World Power Conference in 1929, BMAG presented a locomotive whose boiler pressure blew all conventional and well proven dimensions to the winds. Instead of the usual 200 or 225lbs psi, the boiler pressure of this otherwise conventionally driven 4-6-2 had risen to a utopian 1,707lbs psi. The steam flowed through

A boiler pressure of 1,707lbs psi
Even the layman could recognise the special character of H 02 1001, with its globally unique extreme pressure of 1,707lbs psi. Unfortunately, there were few opportunities to see it from the station platforms as the ambitious experimental locomotive spent more time in the works than in traffic.

Full steam ahead uphill: 01 2066 in the cool of the morning between Munich–Laim and Heimeran Square, 10 December 2016.

Through the efforts of a tireless club initiative, 01 2066 was literally restored from the scrapheap and has enjoyed a quarter of a century of active new life, as seen here on 6 December 2019 in the Munich area. (*Andreas Knipping*)

1. Moving Away from Narrow-Gauge Railways

The railway idyll
The express locomotive enters a bourgeois middle-class Germany – and will contribute to its explosion into the modern era. Here a 'Crampton' shunts in Altona station, of the Altona – Kiel Railway.

Postage stamps

The Deutsche Eisenbahn-Versicherungskasse, originally founded as a self-organising cartel from German railway insurance offices, was active in the field of postage stamps, which have been completely forgotten about today. The stamp showing the famous *Adler* of 1835 was followed by a much enlarged 2-2-2 for local and express passenger trains, although by 1870 the design had already reached its peak.

A steam locomotive in a middle-class area

Even though the legendary *Adler*, built in England for the Nuremberg – Fürth Railway, looked like a 'toy', the two-cylinder 2-2-2 design with its steel boiler, smokebox and tall chimney was a favoured standard for decades. The railway had reached the affluent middle-class areas and would inspire the outbreak of the industrial age.

2. Creative Wheel Arrangements

Phoenix with an express train
There are no colour photographs of locomotives in the nineteenth century. Railway technical expertise and the artistic talent of the painter help us to overcome this deficiency and here we have a realistic vision of a Baden State Railway express train of the 1860s with a well-engineered Crampton engine. The *Phoenix* ran from 1863 to 1890 and stands today in the German Railway Museum in Nuremberg. (*A watercolour painted by Heribert Schröpfer, 1928 – 2017*)

An express at the monastery gate
The street crossing of express trains in Hamburg was another subject for art. The 4-4-0 depicted is from an experimental development of the S 5 family, not an S 3.

Colourful
Before there were colour photographs, technically accurate postcards provide a great source of information. This illustration of the grey/green painted II d with 7ft large red wheels is very lifelike.

The Bavarian Atlantic
The Bavarian S 2/5 of 1904 equipped with slim bar frames and high-pitched boiler, in accordance with modern principles, also embodied the saturated steam system and four-coupled wheel arrangement of earlier traditions. What's more, the unfavourable narrow gap between the rear coupled axle and trailing wheels was a backward step compared with the Baden II d.

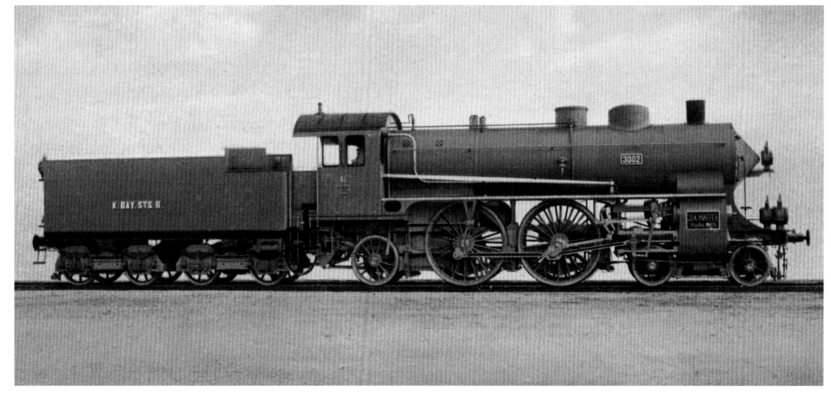

Comparison with the S 3/5
Comparing the two postcards seen here, this particular one shows the S 3/5 (4-6-0) which has the same boiler and many other common features with the S 2/5.

P 4 from the Palatinate
This postcard shows a Palatinate P 4 named after the Bavarian Transport Minister *von Frauendorfer*. From the time when gloss paint made from organic chemicals was utilised without any standardised specification and often with slight ageing, each regional livery could be portrayed in dark grey/ green as well as lush, light green.

3. The Basic European Pattern for the Twentieth Century

Manufactured by Hanomag
The third class of S10s was the three-cylinder S10 2. It is possible that this S10 2 looked as colourful as this in the factory yard of Hanomag. The Reichsbahn painted all of its locomotives black, but painted the frames and wheels red in order to make any cracks more visible.

Railway romance
The queen of Bavarian locomotive development also inspired artists. Admittedly, the S3/6 is seen here on the wrong side of the line in this wildly romantic Alpine scene.

Picture postcard
The wish for a 'Happy Journey into the New Year' has somewhat painful overtones, for in this particular year, 1914, the trains and their passengers were being led into the death and destruction of the First World War. The artist has accurately represented the headlight on the smokebox door as being unlit, as it was not a harbinger of the later three headlight system, but rather a supplementary headlight to indicate when running on the wrong line.

Express in winter
18 477 heads an international luxury train in an inter-war winter. The landscape closely matches the Allgäu route (between Kempten and Lindau), but there was no blue luxury train scheduled on this route. (*A reproduction of a watercolour by Heribert Schröpfer*)

4. Express Locomotives for the Republic and Dictatorship

Standard locomotive as a symbol of value
There was hardly any railway subject depicted in models, drawings or paintings as often as the German standard express locomotive with large smoke deflectors.

100 Jahre Eisenbahn

Accident prevention on the standard locomotives
The standard locomotives were used in the internal training systems of the Reichsbahn's staff. As it was always difficult to see the signals from a steam locomotive's cab, signal positions would be shouted out from the other side. The text on the poster reads, 'Call out signal positions from the other side! Operational safety will be improved!'

Exaggerated celebration of the anniversary
For the 100th anniversary of the first German railways in 1935, the contrast between the euphoric twentieth century and the backward nineteenth century is stressed in this poster, just as the politicians wanted. Thus, the contrast between the modern 01 083 and the first Borsig locomotive of 1841 is very much exaggerated. The text on the poster reads '100 years of the railway'.

Above: Stamps
At times, exotic postal systems fought for the market share of European stamp collectors. Football stars, actors, racing car legends and historic locomotives adorned postage stamps and postcards that were never franked on a letter in the country of issue. Free imagination converted the wine-red German 05 to a light green image in Benin. Meanwhile, stamps of the German State Post Office showed the 05 in a more conventional manner.

Right: Heroic streamliner
This poster of the Henschel-Wegmann train with two admiring young '*Pimpfen*' was created from a mural by Max Teschmacher. (*Pimpfen* was the name given to the junior section of the Hitler Youth movement and means 'little rascals')

Streamline locomotive 03
The maritime painter Walter Zeeden (1891 – 1961) also illustrated many books and magazines with expert railway drawings and in this instance pictured a realistic looking 03.10. This painting shows one of the variations with the streamlining from the coupled wheels and motion removed to improve access for servicing.

Top product in a neighbouring country
Of Germany's neighbouring countries, it was France and Czechoslovakia that dared to build remarkable new locomotives in the post-war years. The colourful paintwork of the Czech 498.022, which was preserved as a museum locomotive, stands in macabre contrast to the gloom that was imposed on the country by the Communists in the year of its construction, 1948. (*Andreas Knipping*)

Above: A reconstructed eight-coupler
We see here the Saxon XX HV in its final form and in all its beauty. In the ten years between their rebuilding in 1964/1965 and their withdrawal in 1974/1976, the pair of 19 015 and 19 022 (latterly class 04) achieved only modest usage. (*Dr Florian Hofmeister*)

Right: 'Reko' locos in Halle
02 0201 and 04 0022 stand next to one another in Halle depot; the latter locomotive is the rebuilt and oil-fired 19 022. (*Dr Florian Hofmeister*)

Above: An express steam locomotive today
In the twenty-first century, the tireless and years-long work of private groups and clubs, rather than the national railway, allows such beauties to return to the track once more, often rescued from scrap. We see here the Bavarian S 3/6 No. 3673 (renumbered back from its DB 18 478) in Lindau during a sunny moment on an otherwise cloudy February day in 2004. (*Andreas Knipping*)

Left: Sunset
And now the evening draws in. The low sun turns the face of 01 2066 golden in this photograph taken between Munich-Moosach and Laim, in December 2016. (*Andreas Knipping*)

Steam train with an S 3/6
Choosing the right spot to photograph the engine working hard on a gradient is less important than travelling on a steam train, so here a telephoto lens has been used to see the Bavarian 'Queen' 3673 on the line from Munich to Lindau, 10 September 2011.

A 're-enactment' on rails
A memorable high point of all special steam train journeys was the run of 01 1066 on 26 April 2015 with the 1950s' timetabled *Roland* from Frankfurt am Main to Kassel and back with its appropriate F-train blue coaches. It ran perfectly to time.

to two high-pressure cylinders and one internal low-pressure one. As the machine was purely experimental, its suitability for everyday working practices could not be known, and despite being given the Reichsbahn number H 02 1001, it was never purchased but instead put into storage in 1934 and scrapped in 1945.

The plausible idea of improving performance and economy by raising boiler steam pressure was pursued by many railway companies. There was a very

significant increase from 60 to 150lbs psi in the nineteenth century, to over 180lbs psi before the First World War, and then up to 200lbs with the most modern former regional state railway engines. Finally, a pressure of around 230lbs psi in the main line engines of the German State Railway's standard locomotives demonstrated the best results. In 1932 Krupp built two Pacifics with a boiler pressure of 355lbs psi. The basic structure and dimensions were kept similar to the 03 so that they could both be

worked on together in the company workshop. In order to make use of the steam pressure increase, the Reichsbahn finally accepted a four-cylinder compound system for the 'medium-pressure locomotives' 04 001 and 04 002. In contrast to the 02, the steam passages and steam chests were increased in size and reduced the internal resistance of the machine. The boilers of the two locomotives were designed differently for experimental reasons. In 1935 they were renumbered 02 101 and 102 because the

The turbine locomotive from Munich
The two turbine locomotives T 18 1001 and 1002 were also unsuccessful. No one today can provide any information about the sound of this Maffei locomotive in action. (*Krauss-Maffei*)

The brand new 03
No one today has the experience of seeing a shiny new express steam locomotive as it left the manufacturer's works, as the 03 223 is doing here. Steam locomotives gained the rails and went into daily traffic far faster than any electric or diesel vehicle. (*Carl Bellingrodt*)

performance was nearer to that of the 01 and 02, rather than, as was expected, that of the smaller 03. Unfortunately, a tragic event ended the active life of the 02 101 when a boiler exploded on 3 April 1939, although this was deemed to be the result of operating error and not high pressure. Sadly, this hindered the further planned development of experimenting with higher boiler pressure on the basis of providing better metal alloys and full welding.

The 03 light Pacific

The systematic development and production of the new standard locomotives levelled out after a few years, and the hectic improvisation of the earlier years faded. The upgrading of bridges and the main lines to take 20-ton axle loads did not happen as fast as expected. As a result, the route network available for the 01 was limited. The financial options were very narrow after the government fulfilled the

distorted war reparation demands of the Western Allies, and were further reduced thanks to the world economic crisis from 1929 onwards. Consequently, in the end the Reichsbahn was forced to purchase the aforementioned Bavarian S 3/6, the last ones of which were delivered by Henschel in 1930 for the west and north German routes. The luxury *Rheingold* express of 1928, run by the Reichsbahn and Mitropa, had to be hauled from Basel to the Dutch border by the Bavarian S 3/6 (18.4-5) and the Baden IV h (18.3), which really looked as if they belonged to a previous era. The Reichsbahn and Locomotive Committee were charged with developing a lighter alternative to the 01 with a 17-ton axle load and sticking with the valued basic principles of the 01, the 03 appeared in 1930. As with the 01, it was available with 2ft 9in and 3ft 3in front bogie wheels, with one-sided and two-sided brakes on the coupled driving wheels and, at the beginning, without with bogie brakes, although these would be added later. They were to become

testbeds for different valve gear and streamlining and just like the 01s, the 03s become both national and international legends. They were undoubtedly classic locomotive beauties and in sensibly chosen fields of operation, namely working the not too heavy expresses in the northern and eastern flat lands, a tremendous success.

The unanimous judgement on the 03 boiler's ability to produce steam was that it was not satisfactory, and in official 'notebooks', its performance was supposedly recorded during test runs. Whilst it was alleged that

the 03 could haul 790 tons on the level at 60mph, and the S 3/6 only 635 tons and the Prussian S 10.1 just 450 tons, in practice, the experience of railwaymen contradicted this. The train crews saw no advantage in acceleration, climbing or fuel consumption with the 03 when compared to the other types that were twenty years older. However, the 03 should not be underestimated as it was later improved in many ways. Ending with 298 units, it holds the top position throughout the world for all steam locomotives running with trains timed at over 60mph.

The view from Bellingrodt's balcony
Whom would we envy more? An unknown traveller on E 337 from Mönchengladbach to Hagen via Düsseldorf and Wüppertal behind the brand new 03 273, or the great photographer Carl Bellingrodt, whose choice of apartment made such images possible from his own balcony? (*Carl Bellingrodt*)

Opposite: **The cathedral bids farewell to an express**
03 072 leaves the busy Cologne main station with the E 53 Cologne – Dortmund semi-fast train. Another train is just departing towards the
four track Hohenzollern Bridge and on the extreme left a local train is forced to wait. Here we have not only reached the era of the 03s, but also
the time of fast shutter speeds that made such sharp pictures possible. (*Carl Bellingrodt*)

Above: **A brand new 04**
Hardly distinguishable from the 01 or 03, the 04 had a boiler pressure of 355lbs psi and a four-cylinder compound system with many additional
innovations. It was a pity that its development was not pursued further. The building of four-cylinder compound and medium-pressure
engines finished in 1932 – 1933 with 04 001-002 and freight engines 44 011-012. Only a Krupp export order to Norway in 1940 once again
demonstrated the strength of this technology. After the Second World War, only France used such types worldwide.

Specialist author, Dr Albert Mühl

Dr Albert Mühl published valuable technical papers at a time when hobby literature for railway enthusiasts did not really exist. In volume 6 – November/December 1961 – of the venerable *Lokomotivtechnik* ('Locomotive Technology') magazine, then celebrating its 85th anniversary, he wrote a profound article entitled 'The Existence and Distribution of Steam Locomotives in 1933', from which excerpts and tables are quoted here. In a historically delicate time, the date 1 April 1933 might not have been noticed at all. When thinking of the year 1933 today, one perhaps thinks less of steam locomotives and more of the nationwide boycott of Jewish shops and the beginnings of the systematic persecution of Jews in Germany. In the history of train transport, the spring of 1933 can be regarded as the eve of the commencement of electric traction from Munich to Stuttgart (1 June 1933). At the same time, it was also the start of express diesel railcars (the regular working of the 'Flying Hamburger' from 15 May 1933).

Now, over to Dr Mühl:

Most of the old regional state locomotives were still in service and the delivery of the standard locomotives was in full swing – there were 13 standard locomotive types compared with no less than 111 regional state locomotive classes. The 743 standard locomotives comprised only 3 per cent of the total fleet of 20,600 standard gauge locomotives – and the fleet in some states still showed an independent character at its core.

By 1 April 1933 there were 100 class 01 locomotives, 10 class 02s and 93 class 03s. The 01s were mainly allocated to depots in northern and central Germany, that is, everywhere where 20-ton axle loads were permitted and where they were needed to haul heavy expresses on difficult routes. In contrast there were just five class 01s in southern Germany at the Offenburg depot, which at that time still had twenty large Baden IV H (18.3s), while ten compound 02s were stationed at the Hof depot. The lighter 03s (17-ton axle load) were only working on the former Prussian network between Königsberg and Cologne, Breslau and Hamburg Altona, being allocated to the lines with weight restrictions and those on the level. For example, the 03s on the Königsberg line worked exclusively on the line from Marienburg to Königsberg and Eydtkuhnen, those from the Altona depot the lightweight express and very fast trains to Berlin, those from Osnabrück from Hamburg to Cologne and the engines at Schneidemühl, from Frankfurt an der Oder and Breslau to Berlin.

Many of the more modern six-coupled former regional state railway classes were still in use. The Prussian 4-6-0s of the S10.1 (17.10) were almost complete, with a large number allocated to depots of the Prussian Division, and were still busy in express work on the level routes. Berlin owned the lion's share, where the S 10.1s were divided between the depots at Anhalt, Lehrter, Gesundbrunnen, Karlshorst and Grunewald and operated a considerable number of the expresses leaving Berlin. The much-reduced number of S 10s (17.0) and the full complement (apart from one) of the three-cylinder S 10.2s were particularly in use in the west and along the Rhine where they were seen, even if only sporadically, on expresses. The S 10s were on their last legs and were being withdrawn. The Saxon XII HV (4-6-0 4-cyl compounds, 17.7) of Dresden Altstadt (Old Town) depot were found mostly on semi-fast services (for example, Dresden – Frankfurt an der Oder) and local and suburban trains, while the Bavarian S 3/5s (4-6-0 4-cyl compounds, 17.4-5) at Nuremberg and Augsburg regularly worked expresses from Nuremberg – Eger, and Nuremberg – Treuchtlingen, as well as Augsburg – Weilheim and Augsburg – Buchloe.

The former state railway Pacifics were still available, apart from the Baden IV fs (18.2). The ten Saxon XVIII H (18.0), the only German three-cylinder Pacific, of the Dresden Altstadt depot ran the express services from Berlin – Bodenbach (Czechoslovakia), Dresden – Leipzig, Dresden – Görlitz –Breslau, and the Württemberg Class C (18.1) of the Stuttgart Rosenheim and Ulm depot ran the expresses to Nuremberg, Munich, Friedrichshafen and Singen. The Baden IV H (18.3) ran on the Rhine Valley route from Mannheim/Heidelberg – Basel, but just a year later they were transferred from Offenburg to Koblenz, Bremen and Hamburg Altona and replaced with another 01. The Bavarian S 3/6 (18.4-5) powered virtually the entire Bavarian express service (from the Munich, Nuremberg, Würzburg, Regensburg, Augsburg and Lindau depots) and were also stationed outside the area at the following depots: Halle, Mainz, Darmstadt and Wiesbaden.

The large Saxon 2-8-2s XX HV (4-cyl compound, 19.0) were based at Reichenbach and Dresden Altstadt in heavy express work on the steeply graded mountain stretches (Reichenbach – Hof and Bamberg, Dresden – Liegnitz, Dresden – Leipzig). The previously mentioned Dresden Altstadt depot was one of the most important express train depots and could easily measure up to Erfurt, Hanover West or Hamm. Finally, the P 10 (39.0), which was almost exclusively allocated to heavy express work, was widespread and could be found in all areas with difficult gradients. They were also very popular in southern German depots and were stationed at Schweinfurt (Würzburg – Schweinfurt - Erfurt), Karlsruhe (Kehl – Stuttgart), Stuttgart-Rosenstein (Stuttgart – Würzburg, Stuttgart – Singen, Stuttgart – Heidelberg). The largest number according to the P 10 diagrams, were in the central German divisions of Dresden, Erfurt, Halle and Kassel. Here they seen at the depots of Dresden Altstadt, Reichenbach, Erfurt,

Eisenach, Saalfeld, Halle, Wittenberg, Leipzig West and North, Göttingen and Paderborn. Further away more were stationed at Frankfurt am Main, Bebra and Magdeburg and also in the Berlin depots at Anhalt and Potsdam. They were not seen on the northern and eastern flat plains of Germany. The P 10s of Jünkerath (Trier Division) travelled the Eifel line and those of Cologne (the depots at Cologne station, Cologne-Deutzerfeld, and Münchengladbach) and those of the Wuppertal Division (depots at Hagen-Eckesey and Wuppertal-Langerfeld) on the hilly routes there. The P 10s of Wanne-Eickel depot (Essen Division) were used for fast goods train traffic. With a total number of 260 locomotives, the P10 was the most widely used express locomotive at the time.

In 1933 the following experimental locomotives were used: both 04 medium-pressure engines were at Hamburg Altona, Krupp's 4-6-2 turbine locomotive T 18 1001 at Hamm, Maffei's T 18 1002 at Munich, and the Schmidt-Henschel high- H 17 206 (60 bar or 876lbs psi), which had been converted from an S 10.2 in 1925.

Allocation of express locomotives on 1 April 1933

Depot	Bw	01	02	03	04	17⁰	17²	17^4/5	17⁷	17¹⁰	18⁰	18¹	18³	18⁴	18⁵	19	39
						Former regional state engines allocated by division only											
Altona						–	–	–	–	15	–	–	–	–	–	–	–
	Altona	–	–	8	2												
Augsburg		–	–	–	–	–	–	25	–	–	–	–	–	21	–	–	–
Berlin						4	–	–	–	44	–	–	–	–	–	–	22
	Anhalter station	10	–	–	–												
	Lehrter station	6	–	–	–												
Breslau						–	–	–	–	20	–	–	–	–	–	–	6
	Breslau main station	–	–	8	–												
Dresden		–	–	–	–	–	–	–	12	–	10	–	20	–	–	23	37
Erfurt						–	–	–	–	–	–	–	–	–	–	–	32
	Erfurt P	18	–	–	–												
Essen						7	–	–	–	17	–	–	–	–	–	–	6
	Dortmund main station	–	–	4	–												

Depot	Bw	01	02	03	04	17^0	17^2	$17^{4/5}$	17^7	17^{10}	18^0	18^1	18^3	18^4	18^5	19	39
	Hamm	15	–	4	–												
Frankfurt						–	–	–	–	–	–	–	–	–	–	–	12
	Frankfurt (M) 1	6	–	–	–												
	Bebra	5	–	–	–												
Halle						27	–	–	–	9	–	–	–	4	–	–	28
	Leipzig main station West	–	–	7	–												
Hanover						–	31	–	–	23	–	–	–	–	–	–	10
	Halberstadt	–	–	6	–												
	Hanover Ost	22	–	6	–												
Karlsruhe						–	–	–	–	–	–	–	20	–	–	–	8
	Offenburg	5	–	–	–												
Kassel						–	–	–	–	–	–	–	–	–	–	–	26
	Kassel	7	–	–	–												
Cologne						14	27	–	–	–	–	–	–	–	–	–	21
	Cologne station	–	–	9	–												
Königsberg						–	–	–	–	11	–	–	–	–	–	–	–
	Königsberg	–	–	6	–												
Ludwigshafen						–	–	–	–	–	–	–	10	–	–	–	
Mainz						5	–	–	–	–	–	–	–	–	25	–	–
Munich		–	–	–	–	–	–	–	–	–	–	–	–	7	5	–	–
Münster						12	9	–	–	–	–	–	–	–	–	–	–
	Osnabrück	–	–	6	–												
Nuremberg		–	–	–	–	–	–	18	–	–	–	–	–	38	10	–	9
Oldenburg						–	–	–	–	6	–	–	–	–	–	–	–
Oppeln						–	–	–	–	4	–	–	–	–	–	–	–
Oppeln						–	–	–	–	4	–	–	–	–	–	–	–
Osten						–	–	–	–	24	–	–	–	–	–	–	–
	Frankfurt/O	–	–	4	–												
	Schneidemühl	–	–	6	–												
Regensburg						–	–	–	–	–	–	–	20	–	–	–	
	Hof	–	10	–	–												
Schwerin						–	–	–	–	8	–	–	–	–	–	–	–
Stettin						–	–	–	–	26	–	–	–	–	–	–	–

Depot	Bw	01	02	03	04	17^0	17^2	$17^{4/5}$	17^7	17^{10}	18^0	18^1	18^3	18^4	18^5	19	39
	Stargard	–	–	4	–												
	Stralsund	–	–	4	–												
Stuttgart		–	–	–	–	–	–	–	–	–	–	37	–	–	–	–	14
Trier		–	–	–	–	–	–	–	–	–	–	–	–	–	–	–	8
Wuppertal																	21
Total		100	10	93	2	48	94	43	12	207	10	37	20	100	40	23	260

Express and long-distance travel between the wars

Before looking at the developments in express locomotives during the politically dark days of the 1930s, let us briefly return to the subject of transport social history. In comparison with the later years of the nineteenth century, long distance travel by rail had obviously become the more natural option. The new elite in business, politics, justice, finance, manufacturing, science, art, media and entertainment had increased dramatically in terms of numbers of people, not to mention their purchasing power, social status and mobility, while the nobility had faded into the shadows. Many engineers, officials, journalists, lawyers or film actors had come from rural backgrounds and therefore made visits to relations in the Sudeten Mountains, the Swabian Alps or the Lüneberg Heath, meaning railway journeys in the summer to their grandparents' house or to get-togethers at Christmastime were always popular. Modern society always demands and promotes new dimensions in mobility, and if conservative reactionaries refused to accept it, the First World War had had a levelling and emancipating effect on the lower classes: office workers, civil servants, technicians and shop assistants, not to mention women in specialist or academic careers, had all experienced great change in their lives, which often meant they travelled to appointments, to further education or to political conferences.

Along with the ordinary expresses, from 1923 onwards a variety of long-distance luxury trains existed in the travel market. Motor vehicles in 1930 were still delicate machines that required constant monitoring and time-consuming maintenance. And then there were the roads! Only a small proportion of the road

An unusual appearance
03s were testbeds for streamlining. Here, 03 154 looks almost alien thanks to a parabolic face over its smokebox door. 03 193 then received full streamlining like the later 05. (*Hermann Maey*)

Swastika fantasies
Producers of historical films like to outdo themselves when it comes to fantasies about the ubiquitous presence of the swastika on railway vehicles between 1933 and 1945. However, only a few locomotives included such images, including the new streamlined experimental locomotive 05 001, seen here during the Summer Olympics in 1936. (*Hermann Maey*)

network was paved, while the rest was merely well-trodden tracks that regularly had potholes and boulders in the way. There were, as yet, no motorways. In every village or small town, the passage of the 'Daimler-Benz', 'Hanomag' or 'Wanderer' could be obstructed by herds of cattle, weekday street markets, horse-drawn carts or closed roads. However, year by year the car was becoming increasingly suitable for everyday use and the manufacturers strove to make compact and affordable vehicles. Meanwhile, wider streets were constructed and made 'clean' thanks to new and different technologies.

Cultural and political emancipation was complete by 1933. Whether at home or travelling abroad, and almost without any effort, the regime managed to instil in the vast majority of the population a sense of nationalist importance in a universe of repression, then rode the crest of the wave to increase production thanks to the later spoils of war. People continued to travel constantly, whether in uniform to portray the empire's deceptive grandeur, or in civilian clothes for business travel – never mind those who were forced into exile as a result of the developing political situation.

The hopes for the streamliners: the 05 and the 61

The global economic upturn of the 1930s was particularly fuelled in Germany by the government's rearmament scheme through its state-ordered financial measures, meaning demand for travel increased further. The fast-running steam locomotives now faced stronger competition, thanks to the creation of the autobahns after 1933, and in the air. There was also further competition on their own lines from the diesel high-speed railcars and the constantly improved electric locomotives. The 03s with improved braking systems could just about be expected to hit 87mph, but even the most dogmatic champion of the two-cylinder locomotives had to see that this would never reach the 95 or 100mph of the E18 electric locomotive or the diesel *Flying Hamburger*.

En route to a basic further modernisation of the railway, the electrification of long-distance routes could have been forced through and the building of high-speed railcars increased. But in the four-year plan announced in 1936 with the goal of self-sufficiency in anticipation of the run up to war, the import of neither the overhead wiring and enough copper for the electric locomotives, nor the oil fuel for countrywide dieselisation were permitted. Coal-fired steam locomotives had to remain the basis for train haulage for the time being.

The Reichsbahn ordered two experimental express 4-6-4 locomotives with 7ft 6½ drive wheels from Borsig, but these were to test modern express carriages rather than for regular high-speed travel. In line with the trends in many other countries, full streamlining over the tender was now required. Designs were shaped after wind tunnel tests and were based on the model of the 03 193, which was used as a design basis. Despite boiler pressure being raised to 284lbs psi with the possibility of multistage use in a compound system, a three-cylinder motion was chosen. The outer cylinders worked the centre axle and the inside cylinder the front-coupled axle. The boiler was compatible with the standard locomotives, with the tube lengths increased to 23ft.

As had been discovered over eight decades earlier, the gasses from tubes less than 12.5ft long were insufficient to heat the water flowing through, and the physics of 1935 were exactly the same as they had been in 1855. This meant that if the tube length was greater than 16ft, any heat generated was used up and therefore any length above this figure was unproductive. It would have been much more intelligent to have enlarged the firebox with a box-like combustion chamber to boost the flames and thereby increase the heat efficiency over the whole heating surface.

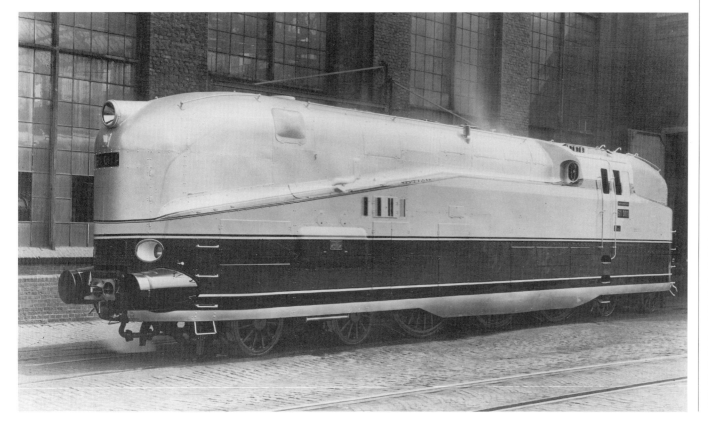

The Henschel-Wegmann train
Had it not been for the rails, the astonished onlooker might have mistaken the seven-axled class 61 for an airship rather than a locomotive. The 61 001 was reserved especially for the Henschel-Wegmann train, which commuted between Berlin and Dresden from 1936 to 1939.

Futuristic look
For the layman, the streamlined mechanically coal-fired experimental locomotive, with its cab at the front, was not recognisable as a steam engine.

The 05's steam production rate was no more satisfactory than that of the 01 or 03. Both engines were delivered in 1935. These wine-red giants, with their vivid representation at exhibitions and in media and films, immediately gained the public's affection. The systematic testing, gradually increasing their way towards the highest speeds, began immediately with 05 002, and it reached 118 and 121mph without any problems. On 11 May 1936 a demonstration run from Berlin – Hanover – Hamburg – Berlin was scheduled with the newest high-speed diesel railcar and the steam locomotive alongside each other. For decades the only

person named as an honoured guest on the special train was Julius Dorpmüller, the transport minister, but today we know that prominent Nazi dignitaries including SS Chief Heinrich Himmler were in the party. Reaching a maximum speed of 125mph between Friesack and Vietnitz, 05 002 travelled the section from Hamburg to Berlin. Never before or since has a steam locomotive gone as fast in Germany or on the Continent, although a British locomotive did reach a slightly higher speed on a slight gradient. American record journeys fail to provide any convincing proof, and so that particular 05 002 can claim to be the fastest steam

locomotive in the world. However, after its record journey it needed a weeklong overhaul with, amongst other repairs, a complete boiler tube replacement. Even after all the test runs, the 05 could by no means prove itself capable of more than 100mph in normal traffic – just the same as the more conventional locomotives. The simultaneous performances of the diesel electric railcars also provided food for thought as they could reach the legendary 125mph (200kph) without preparation or repair work. Weight was also a problem; with its five-axle tender, the 05 weighed 210 tons, a full 50 tons more than the 03 and as much as five standard

express train carriages. Impressed by the success of the diesel high-speed railcars in all types of performance, many engineers and manufacturers (especially Henschel) worked on developing a weight-saving alternative to the steam railcar. But because of the motion's weight and complexity, there was never really a solution when compared with the competition than ran on liquid fuel.

Almost unintentionally comedic was the story of the Henschel-Wegmann train, which entered service between Berlin and Dresden in 1936 with its fully streamlined 4-6-4 two-cylinder engine and the number 61 001, making it the first German express tank engine. As elegant and successful as the violet, cream and silver streamlined train was, it was easy to forget that the industry had initially wanted to pursue a steam-operated lightweight multiple unit. In reality, they now owned a seven-axle tank engine that weighed 128 tons without any coaches and was almost as heavy as a three-car 'Leipzig' diesel unit. Further improvements and strengthening to the three-cylinder 61 002, which had three axles on the rear bogie (a 4-6-6) and had never been seen before – or since – in Germany, led to a total weight of an impressive 144 tons.

The hope of streamlining and mechanical coal firing: 05 003

No matter the locomotive we have discussed so far, not one of them was able to move a metre without the fireman throwing the necessary shovels of coal into the grate. Time and again ideas were put forward and attempts were made to raise the boiler's performance beyond

that which could be achieved with the manual shovelling of coal, and Austria had reported reasonable success with oil-fired locomotives even before the First World War.

In the midst of preparing for war, the Nazis were unwilling to pay expensive exchange rates for imported oil, the fuel needed to achieve higher performance on the rails. Mechanical firing with lump coal was chosen for 05 003. Because the fireman no longer had to take his place between the tender and the fire door, as he had previously, a new bold idea could be entertained: bring the cab to the front to provide good visibility of the track ahead. In this case the boiler was turned round, with the firebox at the front and the driver's controls on the back plate of the cab. With this layout it was necessary to bring the coal forward using a turbo-blower and winding screw through a pipe from the tender alongside the boiler to the front. Unfortunately, it was the unreliability of this system that caused the 05 003 to fail. And it never succeeded in entering regular traffic. As well as its front cab and innovative firing method, the locomotive took its place in German locomotive history thanks to the first use of the hitherto rejected combustion chamber. Its fate in 1945 was also rather peculiar: in the final weeks of the war, it was converted into a standard steam locomotive with the boiler and cab laid out in the traditional manner. The special journeys of the Nazi VIPs, for which this imposing and unique new locomotive was perhaps to be used, no longer took place.

A streamlined hope: the 06

How fast did the main express and luxury trains run in 1935?

In the peaceful years before 1914 there were already several routes, locomotives and coaches authorised for 75mph. This permission did not, however, mean that trains regularly reached this speed, but there was the possibility when trying to regain lost time to exceed the normal 60mph running for short spells. Between the wars, 75mph became the norm, which in turn led to higher maintenance costs for older locomotives. Despite limited funds for investment, trains could be accelerated even during the world economic crisis.

- In 1929 an FD train (FD trains were long-distance fast or luxury trains) was timed at an average speed of over 90kph (56mph) between Hanover and Hamm.
- In 1932 there were five such schedules.
- By 1934 there were no less than 167 runs at more than 56mph, 50 at more than 59mph and 15 at more than 62mph.

The latter speeds were only surpassed in France. For safety reasons, the authorisation for 75mph running required the distance between the pre- and main signals to be increased from 700m to 1,000m in order to ensure sufficient breaking time. It was now necessary to brake the running wheels and to switch from one-sided to double-sided breaking of the drive and coupling wheels. The limited space between the large diameter wheels made this difficult. From 03 163 onwards (with the aforesaid strengthened brakes and increased diameter bogie wheels), the authorised maximum speed was raised to 130 kph (81mph) and after appropriate adaption, the older 03s were also capable of such speed. For the special racing track from Hamburg to Berlin, eleven examples of this class were given dispensation to run at 140kph (87mph) in 1933/1934.

As an important step on the way to higher speeds, the 'Induktive Zugsicherung' (the German equivalent of ATC), or 'Indusi' for short, was essential. Today it is known as 'Punktförmige Zugbeeinflussung' or PZB (literally, 'train location influencing system') and is an integral part of all rail operations. In the mid-1930s, this system of using an electronic signal to ensure compulsory braking if

a stop signal was overrun was extended to the main routes in quick succession.

The experience with the 05, as well as the E18, which at the highest speeds was also not without its problems, the rapid increased expenditure for track improvements, brake technology and signalling systems showed that in the 1930s, the acceleration of train travel across the country to 100mph was not impossible in the long term. Journeys with high-speed railcars, which were heavily advertised and prominent in political propaganda, were just the icing on the cake.

The largest locomotive built in central Europe, the 4-8-4 class

06, was supposed to guarantee a steady 87mph, but the experts at the Krupp manufacturing plant were not particularly enthusiastic about the design. The length of the boiler tubes over the now eight-axled running gear had increased to a grotesque 25ft. In the much too-small firebox, even the most hard-working fireman could not maintain a fire capable of sustaining sufficient temperature over such a length of pipe. And even if the combustion had really been increased to its maximum levels, then the tubeplate at the back of the firebox would have been heated beyond the limit of its metallurgical stability. In these conditions, a shortage of steam

A foreseeable failure
The dreary gigantism of the Nazi era was the stimulus for the building of the 06, which weighed 208 tons with its tender. It failed because of the excessive demands on the fireman to feed its poorly constructed and inefficient boiler.

Class	Number	Speed Increase
17.2 (ex Pr S 10.2)	52	110-120kph (69 – 75mph)
17.10 (ex Pr S 10.1)	125	110-120kph (69 – 75mph)
18.0 (ex Sax XVIII H)	10	100-120kph (62 – 75mph)
18.1 (ex Württ C)	11	100-120kph (62 – 75mph)
18.3 (ex Bad IV h	20	100-140kph (62 – 87mph)
18.4-5 (ex Bav S 3/6)	142	100-120kph (62 – 75mph)
19.0 (ex Sax XX HV)	23	100-120kph (62 – 75mph)
01 from 01 102	still being delivered	120-130kph (75 – 81mph)
02.1	2	120-140kph (75 – 87mph)
03	still being delivered	120-130kph (75 – 81mph)
03	13	120-140kph (75 – 87mph)
03 175 (poppet valves)	1	130-140kph (81 – 87mph)
03 193 (streamlined)	1	130-140kph (81 – 87mph)

Almost at the same time as the 06 another eight-coupled engine appeared, which, with 366 units, was soon to become very useful for express train haulage, namely the class 41, a 2-8-2 with two cylinders and only 5ft 3in coupled wheels.

A special case: Lübeck – Büchen

Three compact, streamlined 2-4-2 tank engines, which were delivered in 1936/1937 by Henschel, together with double-deck push-pull carriages for the Hamburg – Lübeck run of the private Lübeck – Büchen Railway, deserve particular attention. They were the only four-coupled German express steam engines built after the First World War. With the incorporation of the LBE into the Reichsbahn in 1938, and with the beginning of the war a year later, any further noteworthy innovations of

Streamlined engine and double-decker coaches
The smallest German streamlined engine was ordered by the private Lübeck – Büchen Railway. This tank engine, with its new double-decker coaches, was the first step in push-pull working in Germany.

and damage to the firebox and grate occurred, as well as blockage and fracturing of the tubes, all permanent features accompanying both test and regular runs with these two giants. Once again, instead of using the recommended four-cylinder compound system for this class in order to achieve the performance required, the three-cylinder drive of the 05 was retained. Presumably, the railway authorities lost interest in the faulty design even before its delivery and their order in 1936 had to wait until 1939 before its appearance, having been interrupted by the country's rearmament programme and the heavy workload on the locomotive building industry. No one gave it any further thought and the same problems occurred with similar long boilers of the 2-10-2 freight locomotive, the class 45.

A streamlined 01
In 1939, the same year German foreign policy made all thoughts of comfortable express train travel seem light years away, the construction of the last of a series of streamlined locomotives commenced. However, behind its elegant covering hid a mediocre boiler and the fine motion of 01 1088 – and a host of problems. (*Hermann Maey*)

the northern German railway came to an end. Numbers 002 and 003 of these engines, now identified as class 60, were still active, although rather unspectacularly, in East Germany in the 1950s.

Streamlined hopes: the 01.10 and 03.10

More proposals to improve the performance and riding quality of the 01 and 03 were now considered, with three-cylinder drive to increase the maximum speed to 150kph (94mph). However, boilers

for the locomotives in the late 1930s were built to the exact same old principles of the 1920s, with short fireboxes and long boiler tubes. To achieve the required speed, the only modification was the use of streamlining to reduce wind resistance. It was all just old technology under a new, shiny cover: not a good concept for innovation, but unfortunately a typical result of National Socialism.

It could have prompted thoughts for a genuinely modern steam locomotive. In 1932 Krupp had

built two middle-pressure engines, 04 001 and 002, with 355lbs psi and an excellent four-cylinder compound drive. Yet these pressure conditions were not yet manageable with the available boiler materials and welding processes. For example, with a boiler pressure of around 250lbs psi (instead of the 227lbs of the 01 and 03 and the experimental 284lbs of the 05) and improved air access to the firebox, one could have made a decent locomotive.

In accordance with the conservative concept behind the

sheet metal shell, another 55 and 60 examples of the 01 and 03 were built respectively as three-cylinder 01.10s and 03.10s. The appearance of these locomotives was no doubt elegant. In comparison with many foreign constructions, the tender was included in the streamlining, while the lines were tight and without any unnecessary decoration. All the engines were painted black, and so any variations of the 01.10s and 03.10s in red, blue or grey were simply mirages or optical delusions or fantasies of the model railway industry.

With all these streamlined locomotives, disillusionment soon set in as any inattentiveness in operation led to permanent dents in the streamlining cover. Coal dust, flying ash, brake dust, snow, rainwater, autumn leaves, grease and all such debris and dirt collected in the inner recesses, leading to a corrosive mixture which was at risk of catching fire in summer and then freezing in winter. Indeed, some streamlined locomotives took hours to thaw out. The axles and cylinders behind the streamlining

were prone to damage through overheating; inspection, servicing and oiling proved to be very difficult due to the rolling shutters in the earlier versions and was still troublesome in the cut-out panels of later engines. Any leakage from the valves or any part of the boiler, which was easy enough to locate in a locomotive without streamlining, was a mystery when steam was seen escaping from somewhere in the joints of the cladding. Only through the removal of more plates could diagnosis and repair take place.

Clouds of smoke
Poor firing methods seldom happened by chance alone as 01 1088 headed the D 148 from Berlin to Dresden, Prague and Pressburg in the Elbe Valley in Saxon Switzerland. Such clouds of smoke should have been avoided on this stretch of line. (*Werner Hubert*)

Eight cylinders!
The futuristic steam generator locomotive 19 1001 was hardly distinguishable from the 01.10s and 03.10s. On the whole its tests were successful, but wartime conditions and the those immediately afterwards meant that it ran out of time. (*Carl Bellingrodt*)

All these problems would perhaps have been solved by specialist personnel in times of peace, but they quickly became uncontrollable in the war – and it was in wartime that these streamlined engines were delivered. After the Second World War began following Hitler's invasion of Poland in September 1939, the expansion of express train travel into the 'Greater German Reich' was no longer on the agenda. From then on, a reduced number of expresses ran with much heavier loads and priority went to military transport and goods trains which were vital for the war economy. Reliability was now key for operating twelve or fourteen-coach trains at 50 – 60mph, rather than the extravagance of running four coaches at 75 – 90mph.

However, we must not throw the baby out with the bathwater: the streamlined Pacifics possessed excellent running gear and motion, and would be successfully rebuilt in both parts of Germany after 1950.

The last hope for streamliners: 19 1001

In the middle of the Second World War, Henschel completed one of the most interesting German locomotives of the twentieth century, and what is more, it was to be the last genuinely innovative construction this side of the nineteenth century. Externally, the

19 1001 could easily be confused for an 01.10 or 03.10, and it was technically a conventional 2-8-2 with a Krauss-Helmholtz frame and an almost unaltered boiler of the freight class 44. But it was the drive motion that was different. On each side of the locomotive were two steam generators, each in V-shaped arranged cylinders placed alongside steam chests. They worked with a system of linking rods similar to the single-axle drive of the electric locomotives. Any concerns about the weight of conventional valve gear and motion at increasing speeds and the excessive hammer blow on the track appeared to have been overcome. Extensive testing took place until 1943 and although many detailed improvements were necessary, the tests proved that the concept as a whole was practicable.

The ever more difficult war situation made further development impossible. The regular use of the single German steam generator locomotive, which was interrupted many times by visits to the works, ended in 1944. After the war the damaged and decomposing hulk of the locomotive was so interesting to the American experts that it was repaired by Henschel and shipped to the USA on 18 October 1945, where it underwent further tests. However, because interest in steam locomotives died out faster in America than in Europe, the last German streamlined engine was carelessly scrapped in 1952.

Express trains in gloomier times

It is important to remember that even as the 01.10s and 03.10s were being delivered, the war made fast express journeys ever more

Locomotives built by the German State Railway		
Class and manufacturer	Date	Number
4-6-2 2-cyl 01 by Borsig, AEG, Henschel, Hohenzollern, BMAG, Krupp	1926 – 1938	231
4-6-2 4-cyl comp 02 by Henschel, Maffei (rebuilt later as 01)	1925/1926	10
4-6-2 3-cyl high pressure 02 1001 by BMAG (not into DRG traffic)	1929	1
4-6-2 2-cyl 03 by Borsig, BMAG, Henschel, Krupp	1930 – 1937	298
4-6-2 4-cyl comp 04 by Krupp (experimental middle-pressure loco)	1932	2
4-6-4 3-cyl 05 by Borsig (high speed Streamlined loco)	1935	2
4-6-4T 2-cyl 61 by Henschel (streamlined for Henschel-Wegmann-train)	1935	1
4-6-4 3-cyl 05 by Borsig (experimental front cab loco)	1937	1
4-8-4 3-cyl 06 by Krupp (streamlined)	1938	2
4-6-2 3-cyl 01.10 by BMAG (streamlined)	1939/1940	55
4-6-2 3-cyl 03.10 by Borsig, Krupp, Krauss-Maffei (streamlined)	1939/1940	60
4-6-6T 3-cyl 61 by Henschel (streamlined for Henschel-Wegmann train)	1939	1
2-8-2 8-cyl experimental 19 1001 by Henschel (streamlined steam generator loco)	1941	1
Total for the German State Railway (except H 02 1001)		**674**
2-4-2T 2-cyl 60 by Henschel (streamlined tank engine for the Lübeck – Büchen Railway push-pull service	1935 – 1937	3

difficult. The timetable of expresses (D-trains) and luxury long distance trains (FD-trains) was reduced to nothing. Trains of the time were overwhelmingly SF (fast trains for soldiers taking leave from the battle front), SFR (similar but for other journeys) or DmW (expresses with compartments for members of the armed forces). There was no more high-speed running: 50 or 55mph running squeezed between numerous military, supply and essential wartime freights was the order of the day, and was controlled only by telephone or telex to a single local supervisor from a central operating controller and handed over to the driver by means of a form or chalked message

on a blackboard at the signal box, which was only dimly lit at night. One can hardly imagine today how the nightly operations at the stations – as well as daily life for everyone in the cities – could work efficiently in conditions of almost total blackout. Circumstances were adventurous at best during the ever more frequent air raid alerts, turning to apocalyptic when bombs were dropped on the rail network. Trains were cancelled or had to be diverted on a massive scale: the route from Passau to Würzburg might go via Munich, while the route from Berlin to Frankfurt am Main might be via Bamberg. It goes without saying that genuine express locomotives were not required for such operations. On the contrary, the modern mixed-traffic and freight engines of classes 41, 50 and 52 were much better for overloaded trains of moderate speed. Consequently, on 20 September 1944 the transport minister ordered an 'initial' reduction of main and intermediate repairs to a few classes, including the two-cylinder 01s and 03s. This meant the immediate shutdown of all former regional state express locomotives and in the case of the family of Prussian S 10.1s and S 10.2s, these would not return to traffic, at least in the Western Zone. On 22 January 1945 all express trains in what remained of the Reich were cancelled and with it, the works overhaul of the 01s and 03s.

Polish quality
Embarrassingly for the railway managers in the extended 'Greater Germany', the slim 2-8-2 of the conquered and despised Poland performed better in express services than the celebrated streamlined engines. The Pt31 of the Polish State Railway ran in the German State Railway as class 19.1. (*Hermamm Maey*)

Class 486 from Škoda
The development of express locomotives throughout Europe did not stand still between the wars. In 1933 Škoda built this imposing 486 001, a 4-8-2 with three cylinders and 6ft diameter coupled wheels for the Czech Railway (ČSD). Only after the Second World War did the CSD mass produce engines with this wheel arrangement.

Kilometres for the 'Final Victory'

The highest priority was given to the fleet of saloons, sleeping cars, restaurant cars, lavishly equipped in leaders of the 'Third Reich'. In October 1944, luxury for the travelling just that month as the Americans at Aachen and the Russians in East Prussia crossed the borders, the following kilometres of special trains were run for the leading personalities for the purpose of government (from the records of the Ministry of Transport).

Purpose	km
State leader SS Heinrich Himmler (exclusively in the east)	3,174
State Marshal Hermann Göring (exclusively in the north – Brandenburg)	2,932
For state funeral of General Schmundt	1,809
Chief of Transportation General Rudolf Gercke (between Mauerwald HQ and Zossen)	1,452
Upper command of the army	1,426
Fieldmarshal Wilhelm Keitel (exclusively in Silesia)	1,230
Armed forces command	690
Hungarian State Administrator Horthy (Hegyeshalom – Weilheim & return)	1,210
Fighter command (for fighter production)	476
State funeral of Field Marshal Rommel	1,374
Romanian & Bulgarian diplomats	436
Total	**16,409 (10,314 miles)**

However, one should by no means imagine that the constantly deteriorating travel opportunities were offset by a similar decrease in the need to travel. The Nazi regime was still waging a mighty offensive on three fronts (in the east, the west and on the Italian border) and the increasing war in the air required intensive internal organisation to protect this shrinking 'fortress', which meant an extensive mobilisation of people was required. Millions of children were forced out of the bombed cities into the eastern part of the Reich, which was initially less dangerous, under the rubric 'extended child evacuation'. The trauma of flight and displacement later intensified as the situation worsened, and numerous children were torn from their families and swept up into the great westward whirlpool of January 1945.

Chapter 5

FINAL UPTURN AND LATER BRILLIANCE

The German Federal Railway (DB) & the East German State Railway (DR) 'make the best of it'.

The express train in the years of new beginnings

What has been already recorded about the war years was even more acute after Germany's defeat, with travel times and speeds falling back to nineteenth-century levels. Track damage, emergency bridges, rudimentary signalling posts and stations with many lines out of action etc. resulted in numerous slow-speed areas. Furthermore, the need for genuine express locomotives was limited. The frequently overloaded long-distance trains were better served by eight- and ten-coupled locomotives of classes 39, 41, 42, 44, 50 or 52 than the six-coupled engines with large diameter wheels.

The images of trains in those first post-war years remain in the collective memory. There were collections of miscellaneous coaches thrown together, with crowds of people hanging onto the running boards, sitting on the buffers or even the roof.

In the summer of 1945, there were even empty coal trains returning to the Ruhr providing rides to travellers. Standing in an open goods wagon was certainly a macabre novelty, bearing in mind the railway was 100 years old at the time. And in complete contrast to this were a few exclusive trains indicated by the letter 'L' (for 'Luxury') which crossed Germany with international status and were 'for German passengers only with international passes and authorised

Image of destruction
Representing the fate of countless locomotives is 03 1092, which was destroyed after a bomb struck Poznan on 29 May 1944. (*Carl Bellingrodt*)

Above: **A better time is coming...**
Past the ruins of Wuppertal comes the well-maintained 01 1075 with D31, Cologne – Brunswick, in 1949, the founding year of the German Federal Republic. (*Carl Bellingrodt*)

Opposite above: **Timeless beauty**
A gallery of post-war locomotives of the DB. Here 03 1001, 44 1118 and 50 1329 stand ready for duty at the Koblenz-Moselle depot in 1953. (*Carl Bellingrodt*)

Opposite below: **Once a single line**
03 274 hurries through Wilmersdorf station on the line from Stralsund to Berlin via Pasewalk. The railcar travelling in the opposite direction has had to wait because this route, like all main lines of the DR in the former Soviet Zone, was stripped of rails and points, which were taken into the possession of the Russians, and became single tracked. The locomotive has a flat temporary smokebox door.

tickets' or 'barred for travel within Germany', as it was described in the timetable.

For years, many publications about German railway history would say that few people travelled in these poor economic conditions, yet the opposite was the case. The mobilised society created by the war had now turned into an uprooted society during the occupation. Millions of liberated forced foreign labourers, prisoners of war and political detainees now wanted to make their way to a new life.

Millions of Wehrmacht or Waffen SS members were gradually released from captivity or internment, or left hospitals and made their way home to relatives, which was hard enough because so many families whose homes had been bombed had found shelter elsewhere. More forced travel situations arose because of the flight or expulsion of Germans from Poland, Czechoslovakia, Hungary and Yugoslavia and from the former German territories east of the Oder and Neisse rivers.

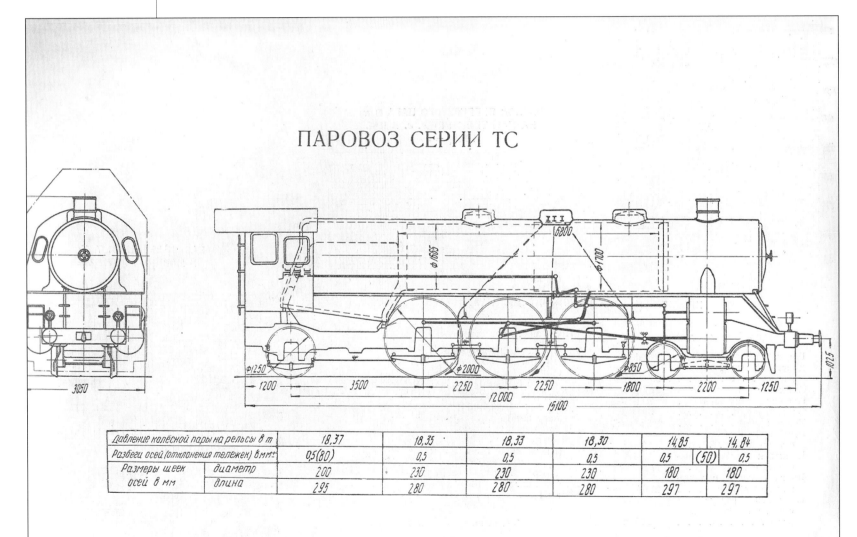

ПАРОВОЗ СЕРИИ ТС

Давление колёсной пары на рельсы в т		18,37	18,35	18,33	18,30	14,85	14,84
Разбеги осей (отклонения тележек) в мм±		0,5 (80)	0,5	0,5	0,5	0,5 (50)	0,5
Размеры шеек осей в мм	диаметр	200	230	230	230	180	180
	длина	295	280	280	280	297	297

Soviet weight diagram

The military collapse in 1945 meant that German railway vehicles were left in around fifteen countries. Twenty examples of the Reichsbahn's 03 were put into service in Lithuania as class TC and the drawing opposite provided the Soviet engineers with an overview for their rebuilding.

Express trains started again on 22 September 1945 between Munich, the largest town in the American Zone, and Frankfurt am Main, which was the zone's administrative centre. The first timetable for the US Zone, valid from 1 January 1946, showed a journey time of 10 hours and 6 minutes for this D 369 service! It travelled via Kornwestheim and thus bypassed Stuttgart's main station.

American/British military traffic between the western zones and Berlin began on 20 November 1945, but these did not appear in the timetable. On the other hand, the first international express open to the general public was inaugurated on 1 October 1946 between Amsterdam, Hanover, Helmstedt and Berlin, and certainly generated a lot of public interest.

There were also new train classifications: DBA trains were for the British armed forces, DFA for the French and DUS for the American. The trains used by the Soviet army were not in the public timetable. Strangely enough, trains reinserted into the timetable in the western zones were identified anachronistically as 'DmW'.

De-streamlined and stripped of parts
The lower half of the streamlining of 05 002 was sacrificed not as a direct consequence of the war, but a practical requirement in service. After several years' storage it was found in this condition at the Krauss-Maffei Works in Munich awaiting overhaul. (*Dr Scheingraber*)

'With nothing below' in the Western Zones
In the short time in which the Reichsbahn was supervised by the four occupied zones, the partially de-streamlined express locomotive 01 1052 is seen hauling D 90 near Wernfeld, en route from Hamburg Altona to Munich via Würzburg. The first vehicle is an ancient wooden Prussian express carriage. (*Carl Bellingrodt*)

...and in the Eastern Zone
A comparable picture shows 03 1010 on East Germany's railway.

Streamlining brought into line
61 002 had full streamlining. Political slogans were ever present and absurdly plastered over locomotives and station buildings in the Soviet-occupied zone. None of the disempowered citizens of the so-called German Democratic Republic had any possibility of banning the atom bomb or enforcing world peace in any way (as urged by the slogan on the side of the engine)!

It is worth comparing typical express journey times on the main routes for the last pre-war timetable, the last published timetable of 3 July 1944, and then the three post-war summer timetables.

Comparison of journey times, 1939 – 1956

Route	1939	1944	1946	1949	1956
Berlin – Hamburg Altona	3.31	4.46	No service	6.36*	7.04*
Berlin – Hanover	3.31	4.47	No service	7.34*	6.41*
Cologne – Hamburg	6.36	7.53	10.31	7.34	6.23
Munich – Frankfurt (Main)	6.08	7.59	10.15	7.51	6.01
Dresden – Leipzig	1.40	2.19	2.54	2.54	2.25
Berlin – Dresden	1.56	3.19	5.24	4.06	3.57
Basle – Karlsruhe	2.34	3.41	5.43	4.40	3.30

* The time from Berlin to Hamburg & Hanover included border customs control of 101 minutes in Schwanheide and 79 minutes in Marienborn – in 1956 it was 57 and 60 minutes respectively.

01 1057 on the blue
Rheingold Express
The introduction of the
overhauled 01.10 and
03.10 locomotives in the
early days of the Federal
German Railway (DB)
has a special place in
German railway history.
The heavy D-trains
and the ambitious
F-trains introduced
in 1951 demanded
performances that were
hardly ever required
either before or since.
Here we see 01 1057
in Offenburg in 1952
on the F 164 *Rheingold
Express* from the Hook
of Holland to Basel. At
the time, the train had
blue 'apron carriages'.
(*Carl Bellingrodt*)

**Portrait with a
distinctive feedwater
heater**
A closer view: the former
streamlined 01 1088
with its characteristic
cylindrical feedwater
heater. (*Carl Bellingrodt*)

The 'blue wonder' engine
The de-streamlined 03.10 was one of the most handsome German steam engines. 03 1014 was, at this time, painted blue and carried decorated polished boiler rings. (*Carl Bellingrodt*)

Sorting out and overhaul: express locomotives in the 'bad times'

In my generation, born in the early years after the Second World War, there was a fixed idea about the 'bad times' that involved parents telling their children about their struggles to purchase the bare minimum of food, not to mention the Berlin Blockade, when a few raw potatoes were sent to the beleaguered western sector of Berlin in registered parcels.

Countless locomotives rusting in sidings in various stages of disrepair and from all over the country formed the picture at many train stations. But there remained

an understandable resignation to the apocalyptic situation and so a great clean up followed by a massive rebuilding programme began. Cooperation with the occupying powers functioned smoothly, with the Soviet military administration working on the principle that one hand did not know what the other was doing. Whereas on the one hand, almost from the first day, the building of a communist allied state was being forced into existence, on the other hand the production capacity and infrastructure of that future partner was being ruthlessly dismantled. Germany's administration and economy, and thus also its railways,

were pretty poor in 1948, but were at least in an organised state: no one travelled on locomotive tenders, in goods wagons, on the buffers or on carriage running boards any more.

As far as locomotives were concerned, conditions were very different in the four zones. Because many locomotives had already been moved westward in the last phase of the war, the British and American zones had more locomotives than they needed. In contrast, the locomotive fleet in the French Zone was barely sufficient and the Soviet Zone had a major shortage because so many machines had been moved westwards before the end of the war, never mind the massive attacks

The Rhine is beautiful here
What a glorious train! 03 1022 is pictured here with E 714 and a couple of double-decker coaches of the Lubeck-Buchen Railway (LBE). It is passing the Burg Rheinstein (Castle Rheinstein) on its journey from Dortmund to Frankfurt am Main in 1951. (*Carl Bellingrodt*)

The new European carriage museum: a heavy load for 03 1051
03 1051, taken in 1950 near Trechtinghausen on the Rhine, has a harder task on the FD 163 Basel – Hook of Holland express. (*Carl Bellingrodt*)

The *Rheingold Express* runs again
The first post-war *Rheingold* on 20 May 1951. 03 1051 is near Bacharach with shining, restored blue carriages and silver roofs. Passengers were businessmen, officials, officers of the occupying powers and members of parliament, which for the previous two years had been located in Bonn. The empty road alongside seems like a fairy tale to us today. (*Carl Bellingrodt*)

conducted by the Allies on the rail network. Quite apart from those taken further east, for many years the remaining higher-performance engines were taken into the so-called column service of the military, or as war reparations by the occupying power as far as the Polish – Soviet border. The relaxed situation in the western allied zones meant that almost all the multi-cylinder express locomotives, and thus almost all the large-wheeled former regional state railway engines, were decommissioned. Hardly any of the

class 17s stored at the end of the war returned to steam, which was in total contrast to the Soviet Zone, where locomotives of classes 17, 18 and 19 remained indispensable for a long time. In all the zones the 01s and 03s formed the nucleus of the express locomotive fleet; the problems with the streamlining having already been eliminated before the collapse. The 01.10s, 03.10s and 05 were released from their disintegrating metal covers, given conventional boiler lagging and added to the regular operating fleet. The major

overhaul of a DB 03.10 lasted four and a half months on average, while the general overhaul of a sister locomotive on the East German DR took more than twelve months. The contrasting economic situation in the two Germanys would last a long time. In the West, cast, welded or rolled steel, copper and brass, rubber and grease were expensive, but were readily available without any limit both internally and as imports, while the East had to rely on a much narrower availability of assets and materials.

The world record locomotive de-streamlined
Among the most impressive locomotives of the young DB were the three restored 05s. The world record holder, 05 002, emerged from the Krauss-Maffei Works in 1951 after a long stay. (*Carl Bellingrodt*)

05 003 was also de-streamlined
The 05s were also preferred for hauling F-trains. Here, 05 003 is heading the F 14, the *Dompfeil* (literally the *Cathedral Arrow*) from Hanover to Cologne, near Gruiten. The end for these proud beauties came quickly: with their already reduced boiler pressure, the non-standard class of three fell victims to the V 200 diesels in 1958.

The two failed giants of the 06 class remained stored by the DB and were scrapped. This led to the somewhat curious result that after the Second World War, the only streamlined engines left were tank engines, namely 61 001 (until November 1951) in the West and 60 002, 60 003 and 61 002 in East Germany. A further observation regarding the huge renovation in the difficult post-war years is that the late technical history of German express locomotives is actually a story of successful rebuilding and only a minimal number of new constructions.

The DR's large smoke deflectors

No 01.10s remained in the DR fleet, so the renovation of the streamlined locomotives for the eastern network was limited to the 03.10s. Large smoke deflectors created an appearance similar to that of the two-cylinder 01s and 03s. Here, 03.1046 awaits departure from Leipzig.

AVAILABLE EXPRESS LOCOMOTIVES AT THE END OF 1950 IN THE WEST AND EAST

Class	DB	DR
01	165	65
01.10	54*	-
03	144	80
03.10	26**	19***
05	3****	-
17.10	-	45
18.0	-	9
18.1	25	-
18.3	3	1
18.4-5	86	-
19	-	21
60	-	2
61	1	1

　　* renovated March 1949 – May 1951
　　** renovated February 1949 – November 1950
　　*** general overhaul April 1952 – December 1954
**** renovated October 1950 – April 1951

The DB's large smoke deflectors

The standard locomotives of the DB retained the large smoke deflectors of the pre-war Reichsbahn. This photograph of 01 230, taken in 1951 in the station of Wuppertal-Elberfeld, still without glass in the roof, is a reminder of the immediate post-war period. (*Carl Bellingrodt*)

Nothing new in the East

The DR kept the old smoke deflectors so that 01 120 is seen here on 26 June 1967 in Berlin's Ostbahnhof (East Station) in its traditional appearance. (*Locomotive driver Günter Meyer*)

Blank space for slogans
The large smoke deflectors seemed the ideal place for political propaganda. In this image from 1960, 01 186 highlights to onlookers in Berlin that they were under the care of the 'German-Soviet Friendship Brigade'.

Above left and above right:
Abused for propaganda
03 195 is somewhat overladen with messages at the delivery of the 3,000th overhaul at the 'Wilhelm Pieck' Works in Chemnitz in 1951. The president of East Germany and other officials are greeting the World Festival Games in Berlin and the people's friendship. A wooden tablet with Gothic script on the side of the boiler reads 'Railwaymen stand guard for peace', that is to say: they will take part in the build up of the armed forces, which had already begun.

Right: **Peaceful rest**
The scene is very peaceful with an 03 in Berlin's Friedrichstrasse (Frederick Street) station. Only in this part of the divided city was it possible to see an express coming from the East, completing its journey, and the train engine drawing the empty carriages away tender first. Shortly after, in 1961, the eastern part of the inner city border station of Friedrichstrasse was screened with high walls (the Berlin Wall).

Berlin, Bahnhof Friedrichstraße

Express locomotives in Cologne

Back in the West! Like Dortmund, Hamm, Hanover, Hamburg, Bebra, Frankfurt and Mannheim, Cologne was a centre of operations for express steam locomotives. Photographs like this could have been taken at the foot of the cathedral at any time of day – as here on 4 October 1957 with 03 074 (for a train from Mönchengladbach to Frankfurt), 01 122 (Krefeld to Basle) and a further unidentified 01.

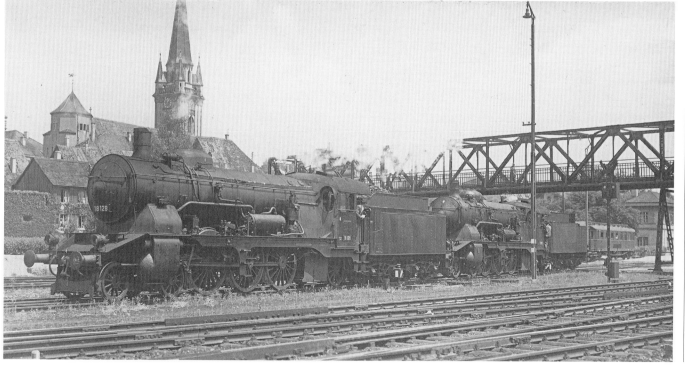

Still former regional state railway engines

Alongside more or less modernised standard Pacifics – and ever more electric and diesel engines – there remained some former regional state railway classes in their regional home territories. The Württemberg Cs with the numbers 18 128 and 18 102 are waiting in Radolfzell for their next turns. (*Carl Bellingrodt*)

Elegant 'witte' smoke deflectors

It goes without saying that both the DB and DR adjusted their huge locomotive fleets to requirements with the technology available. The welding of the boilers instead of riveted joints was not visible externally. The DB replaced the large smoke deflectors with 'witte' deflectors. We note that 03 064 is also fitted with Indusi magnets, and it has kept its small bogie 7,000-gallon tender, which was advantageous for short turntables.

Combustion chamber and feedwater heater

An intermediary step towards more capable boilers was the fitting of five 01s with combustion chambers and feedwater heaters in 1950. The well-maintained 01 154 stands ready for departure at Munich. (*Dr Günther Scheingraber*)

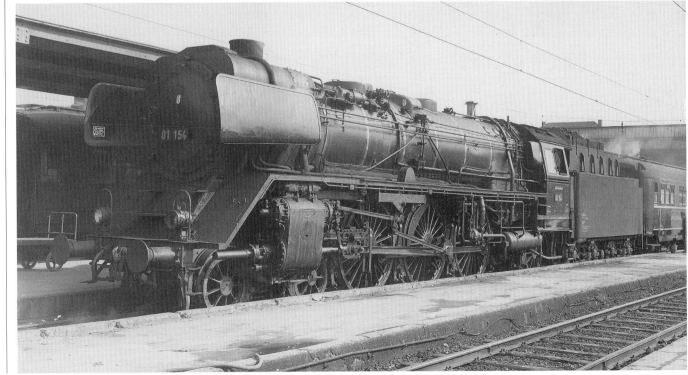

True beauty!
This 03 really does have an elegant appearance, and the small smoke deflectors strengthen the impression of lightness. A certain amount of literary controversy about the 03s flared up in the DB period, in which the standard locomotives were discounted. In the end, limited improvements such as the welding of boilers and improvement to the draughting with narrower blastpipes made the 01s and 03s very useful express engines for the years between their renovation and electrification. (*Helmut Först*)

A haven of calm from the hustle and bustle
Right in the middle of post-war society, 03 170 stands in the soft light of the main hall of Hamburg-Altona station. The era of the steam locomotive was coming to an end, but in 1974 the demolition of the hall at Altona, originally constructed in 1889, was a sin of misguided ideology. (*W. Brauns*)

Necessity is the mother of invention: the S 10.1 fired with pulverised fuel

All the locomotives described up until now were fired with hard coal from the Ruhr area, the Saar basin or the coalfields of Upper Silesia, with the single exception of 05 003, which was fired with lump coal from the mechanical stoker. East Germany had no hard coal deposits to speak of. It was less the much-rumoured malice by the capitalist West than the self-inflicted trade restrictions of the Stalinist economic system which prevented access to the Ruhr coal on the other side of the border, or the coal of Upper Silesia in what is now Poland. Consequently, the development of the supply of East German brown coal for every type of heating was driven forward as the highest priority. Hans Wendler had developed a system of pulverised coal firing for locomotives based on tests conducted during the inter-war period. Using surprisingly simple technology, the fuel was drawn by suction from the tender into the firebox of the steam engine. In addition to goods engines, fourteen locomotives of the 17.10 class (ex Prussian S 10.1s) were thus rebuilt between January 1950 and January 1955, as well as 03.1087 and two special engines, namely 07 1001 and 08 1001 in 1952. The former was 231 E 18 of the French Nord Railway, a four-cylinder compound 4-6-2, and the latter 241 A 4, of the French Est Railway, a four-cylinder compound 4-8-2. Both had been among the considerable number of locomotives that the Germans had taken with them when they

A DR locomotive with pulverised fuel
The firing of steam locomotives with pulverised coal remained a historical event. This photograph from 1951 shows 17 1042's adapted tender. See how its crew have been 'tanned' by working with this new fuel.

withdrew from France in 1944. In any case, neither of these was satisfactory in service and after a modest performance they were stored on 1 March 1957 and scrapped a year later. However, the concentrated allocation of the 17.10s to Cottbus developed in a more satisfactory way and they were stored between November 1957 and August 1962, with the main reason being the overall condition of the machines rather than any problems with the pulverised fuel firing. The Achilles' heel of this new style of firing was typical of East Germany: the industry could not maintain or even increase delivery of the brown coal in the fine-grained form needed. There were, however, other problems. The pulverised fuel locomotives had no ashpans, and all unburned remnants of the fine coal went up through the chimney. Consequently, the use of pulverised fuel created an intolerable pollution of the locomotives, rails and the surrounding area.

The last flower of the compound locomotive: the S 3/6 with new boiler

A German speciality that was unique in the world was the equipping of many classes with new boilers. In the case of the latest series of the Bavarian S 3/6, it was not the failure of the existing boiler to produce sufficient steam but the wear and tear and worn-out parts that resulted in the decision to provide thirty of the class with all-welded new boilers with combustion chambers. Naturally, the rebuilding was combined with other improvements. The management of the Minden HQ office and the Krauss-Maffei company managed to preserve the harmonious form of the ongoing S 3/6. Between 1953 and 1957 more class 18.6 came into service, but their use in the states of Hesse and Bavaria, and finally on the Munich Augsburg – Lindau route ranged from just five to eleven years. Electrification made so many modern standard locomotives available that the rebuilt engines, which were subordinate in terms of speed and power, became disposable far too early. The rest fell as victims to dieselisation.

New construction of old regional state railway engines
The layman could hardly recognise the strengthening of the S 3/6 with the new boiler, because the basic structure and appearance were preserved. The use of the class number 18.6 was, admittedly, alarmingly short, and they shared the fate of many good locomotives built in the 1940s and 1950s.

Above: **All roads lead to Paris**
An 18.4 (ex Bavarian S 3/6) passes alongside Lake Constance and will soon reach Lindau. The kilometre signpost to Paris, Innsbruck and Strasbourg is reminiscent of the time when Lindau was occupied by the French, as was south Württemberg and the Vorarlberg Alps.

Right: **S 3/6 variants**
On closer inspection, the three almost identical faces of the S 3/6 reveal the difference between 18 538 on the left, the 18.6 with the bigger newbuild boiler in the middle, and one of the last 18.4s still extant in the year this photograph was taken, 1958.

A second renovation of the three-cylinder locomotives

No sooner had the DB and DR brought their long-stored streamlined 01.10s and 03.10s back to life as express locomotives with a regular design, and with considerable effort, when they were confronted with a well-known design weakness from their earlier days: the choice of material. The streamlined classes (as well as a number of conventional standard locomotives of the 41 and 50 classes) were equipped with long boilers of the steel grade St47K, the 'K' standing for 'cold-rolled'. The steel was harder than the earlier boiler steel, meaning weight could be saved using a lower thickness, which was necessary in view of the additional load caused by the third engine and fairing.

Unfortunately, the material became brittle after a short time due to the nitrogen that remained in the steel following the heavy rolling process. The lack of elasticity lead to cracks, which resisted any welding repairs. Attempts were made to lengthen the life of the boiler by using patches of conventional St34 steel, and constant checks were made to avoid the risk of an explosion.

Only briefly in service
The modernisation of the 03.10 came too late to be of any importance for train operation. They worked between Aachen and Helmsted for only a decade. 03 1017 is here, recently rebuilt.

THE REGIONAL ALLOCATION OF EXPRESS LOCOMOTIVES:
01 – 19 and 39 and 41 working relevant D-trains in Germany, 1955/1956

SOUTH REGION, 3 JUNE 1956

District	Depot	Class
Augsburg	New-Ulm	39
	Kempten	39
	Lindau	18.5
Frankfurt (Main)	Frankfurt (M)	01, 39
	Giessen	39
	Dillenburg	39
	Wiesbaden	03
	Darmstadt	03, 18.6
Karlsruhe	Heidelberg	39
	Karlsruhe	39
	Offenburg	01, 01.10
	Villingen	39
	Konstanz	38.10
Kassel	Kassel	01.10
	Bebra	01.10
Mainz	Ludwigshafen	03, 03.10
	Kaiserslautern	39
	Coblence-Moselle	01
Munich	Treuchtlingen	01
Nuremberg	Nuremberg	18.6
	Würzburg	01
Regensburg	Regensburg	18.5
	Hof	01, 18.5/6
Stuttgart	Stuttgart	39
	Ulm	18.4
Trier	Trier	38.10

(still without the Saar railways)

WEST REGION, 22 MAY 1955

District	Depot	Class
Essen	Hamm	01, 05
	Dortmund	03.10
	Paderborn	23
Hamburg	Hamburg Altona	03, 03.10
	Lübeck	41
Hanover	Hanover	01, 03
	Bremen	03
	Brunswick	01, 41
Cologne	Cologne	01,03
	Cologne -Deutz	03, 23
	Mönchengladbach	23
Münster	Osnabrück	01.10, 03
	Rheine	03
Wuppertal	Hagen-Eckersey	01, 01.10, 41
	Siegen	23

Daily average diagrams of more than 800 Km (500 miles) undertaken by 01s of Hanover (818km) 01.10s of Osnabruck (874km) and 03.10s of Dortmund (1,053km).

With new boiler
The new boiler turned the rather unfortunate streamlined 01.10 into a very capable German steam locomotive. We see here 01 1060 freshly turned out after it renovation on 4 December 1953. (*Carl Bellingrodt*)

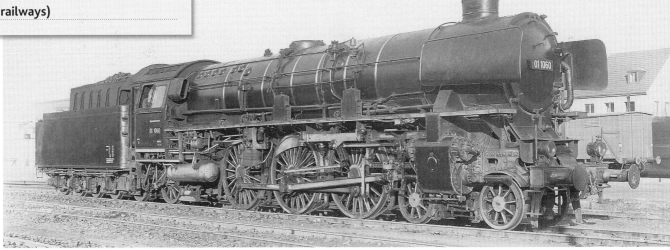

DR ALLOCATION, 1 JULY 1955

District	Depot	Class
Berlin	Berlin East	03
Dresden	Dresden Old Town	18.0, 19, 39
	Gera	39
	Karl-Marx Stadt	39
	Karl-Marx-Hilbersdorf	39
	Reichenbach	39
	Riesa	39
	Zwickau	39
Cottbus	Cottbus	17.10
	Görlitz	39
Erfurt	Erfurt	01
Greifswald	Stralsund	03.10
Magdeburg	Magdeburg	01
Schwerin	Wittenberge	01
Halle	Halle	03, 03.10, 18.3
	Leipzig West	03

Left: **Without any decoration – and still handsome**
The beauty of technology! The face of Brunswick's newly rebuilt 01 1061 in the sunshine of January 1954, with the protruding tail-rod cover of the three-cylinder locomotive. (*Carl Bellingrodt*)

Below: **With the feedwater heater on the upper surface**
The 03.10s on the DR were at risk of boiler explosion and were the first of the standard Pacifics to be rebuilt with a new boiler. 03 1010, which was based at Halle research centre for many years, received a feedwater heater on the top of the smokebox. (*Gerhard Illner*)

Problems initially came to a head with the particularly heavy 01.10s of the DB. Just over two years after their return to traffic, new boilers had to be procured from Henschel and were fitted between December 1953 and October 1956 so that they could be reliably used on the most strenuous turns. In the meantime, the installation of a combustion chamber and full welding of the boiler had become a matter of course, while the equipping with a feedwater-heater was also an innovation. From then on, the 01.10s achieved the best performances in the history of German steam locomotives on the north – south route from Hanover to Würzburg/Frankfurt am Main, until the line's electrification in 1963.

A crack in the long boiler of 41 229 during a hydraulic test of only 165 lbs psi on 28 April 1955 revealed the seriousness of the situation with this class, as well as the 03.10s with the same boiler. In this instance, the DB decided to reboiler. Roller bearings on the outer driving and coupled rods and a mechanical coal pusher in the tender with a cover over the coal bunker were additional innovations. Unfortunately, there was little joy in the operation of the superheated steam regulator.

Right: 03.10 of the DR
Nearly all new-build and reconstructed locos (*Rekoloks*) of the DR received a feedwater heater with the characteristic 'trapeze' profile above the smokebox, seen here on 03 1048 at Stralsund depot on 25 August 1969. (*Max Delie*)

Below: Another 03.10 of the DR
03 1010 has been preserved as an operational museum locomotive and has run countless special and 'planned' trains over the last three decades, as here in 1991 on the Berlin – Magdeburg line. (*Andreas Knipping*)

construction capacity and the necessary financial capital in East Germany. Knowing what was required, two new-build boilers were constructed in 1957 to the old pattern. When the up-to-date new boilers with combustion chambers were at last produced as a series, the class 39 2-8-2s were reconstructed from the spring of 1958 and reclassified as class 22. The principle of 'hope' had to suffice for the 03.10's dangerous boilers, but in the last minutes of 30 September 1958, the journey of D 78 from Berlin to Prague and Vienna via Dresden came to an abrupt end when the boiler of 03 1046 exploded. The driver was killed immediately, while the fireman survived with severe injuries.

Apart from the two examples already equipped with the 1957 boilers, the whole class was stored in the first week of October 1958. Between February and December 1959, sixteen of the renovated 03.10s were equipped with new boilers built at Meiningen and rejoined their two colleagues that already had them. With many other innovations, the railway virtually gained a new class, although the shortage of different parts to finalise the boilers and other teething problems still needed to be addressed.

Permanent guests in the express fleet: the old 39 and the new 22

As has already been noted, in the twenty-five years from 1920 to 1945 the Reichsbahn had built no eight-coupled express locomotives apart from the two curious giants of class 06. Therefore, the Prussian

Maintenance work
No wheel will turn without the hard work of the driver, fireman and shed staff. The crosshead and slide bar of 03 1089 are being oiled in Stralsund depot, August 1969.

The risks caused by the St47K steel used in the boilers was just as well known in the East as in the West. Boilers were patched, welded, and monitored, and in 1955, leading committees reached an agreement regarding the reboilering of the 03.10s. But, ten years after the war, what was a welcome order for a host of locomotive manufacturers in West Germany turned into a year-long struggle for materials,

The 'nearly' express locomotive of class 22
With the conversion of the failing parts of the class 39 to form a new class 22, the DR improved the availability of its express train services considerably, and it was a pity that electrification and dieselisation meant they had a very short heyday. Reichenbach's 22 030 is seen here turning around in Hof on 25 July 1964. (*Hans Schneeberger*)

P 10 and DRB class 39 were indispensable both during the war and afterwards. The DB was gradually able to relieve the strain on some of the 'old ladies' (the Württemberg and Bavarian Pacifics of the century's first decade) with the gradual electrification of many routes in south-west Germany, and also actioned many large rebuilding projects. The DR, on the other hand, remained absolutely dependent on the 39s for use in the low mountain ranges of the Erfurt and Dresden districts. The difficulties of obtaining good combustion and generating steam were increased with the necessary forced use of brown coal briquettes. And on top of all that, the boilers were also showing signs of fatigue. It was therefore decided to undertake a comprehensive reconstruction

of the entire existing structure on the same lines as the 03.10s – with the same modern boiler and combustion chamber. Accompanied by the provision of new cylinders, driver's cab and the attachment of a standard tender, the remodelling was so extensive that – with a somewhat hesitant glance at the frame, wheels and motion – a new class number was given in the series retained for standard locomotives. Between May 1958 and March 1962, the 'freshly-baked' 22 001 - 22 085 left the Meiningen Works, and operation with the 'Rekoloks' was overall satisfactory. From the first days, the higher demand required in service and made possible by the new boiler was, admittedly, accompanied by a noticeable increase in damage to the older running gear. As a result, and also

because of further electrification in the south of the DDR, the class 22 was withdrawn from service between 1967 and 1971. Fifty-two of their good boilers were transferred to the standard locomotives of class 03 between 1969 and 1975, which increased their reliability and performance considerably in their last years in service.

Class 10: the 'Black Swan'
Almost as a matter of course, the railway authorities in both parts of the divided Germany quickly turned their thoughts to the construction of new steam locomotives soon after 1945, as nationwide electrification based on the Swiss model initially seemed just as utopian as the total transition to diesel that was seen in the United States. With the loads

and speeds laid down in plans for both East and West Germany, it was not surprising to consider an express locomotive with multi-cylinder drive for the interim period. This concept was soon put to one side in East Germany because their political values and poor economic circumstances meant priority was given to freight and commuter traffic in many areas. In West Germany, development work was struck by indecision. While a 2-6-2 (class 23) in the form of an advanced development of the already delivered mixed traffic and local passenger engine was considered sufficient, an imposing 4-8-2 was considered next. Ultimately, a decision was made

for a three-cylinder 4-6-2. Finally, an order was placed at Krupp to deliver two examples of the class 10. However, during its long construction period the transport minister and the DB authorities lost interest in steam locomotives.

The large diesel hydraulic locomotive, the V 200, which was suitable for express work, went into series production in 1956 and the electric E 10 followed in 1957. The 10 001 and 10 002 were also delivered that same year. With a partial streamlining in the area of the cylinders and with a skirt under the running plate, the 'black swans' were the last new steam locomotives for the German railways, their

conspicuous appearance arousing both enthusiasm and some head-shaking. The class 10 was a very modern engine, with an all-welded boiler and combustion chamber and roller bearings on all running parts. It was also the most powerful of all newly built or converted German express steam locomotives. Not so satisfactory, however, was its very substantial weight. With an axle weight of 22 tons, it was limited to just a few routes. Subject to frequent failures and unpopular with its crews, it supplemented the stock of the 01.10s on the north – south route between Kassel and Frankfurt am Main. The curtain fell on its activities after only a decade, in 1968.

The latecomer
The last German express steam locomotives of class 10 were controversial both technically and aesthetically. Although it was only ten years old, 10 002 would soon bid an early 'farewell' at Treysa in September 1966. The overhead wires for the Frankfurt am Main – Kassel electrification were already in position. (*Gottfried Turnwald*)

Class 10s built	
DB	Number
4-6-2, 3-cyl by Krupp, 1957	2

When it comes to 'new build' construction, one cannot avoid mentioning that both the DB and DR initially liked to use their mixed traffic engines of class 23 (built 1950 – 1959) and the 23.10 (1956 – 1959), both two-cylinder 2-6-2s with 105 DB and 113 DR examples that were often put into express service. Their maximum speed of 110kph (69mph) was good enough for many routes in the post-war conditions.

Later giants elsewhere

It is now time to take a look over Germany's borders, and the late importance of the 4-8-2 wheel arrangement is noticeable. The Czech three-cylinder 4-8-2s of classes 498.0 and 498.1, with fifty-five examples built between 1948 and 1955, were very successful. At the peak of international locomotive construction before 1945 was the French 4-8-2. Indisputably, the crown was worn by four-cylinder compounds with 6ft 8in driving wheels, classified 241 P, of which thirty-five were delivered between 1948 and 1952. As well as the Czechs, the French also reduced the work of the fireman by a system of mechanical firing, which was sometimes known in Europe by its American name of 'stoker'.

But things got even bigger! After the Second World War the Soviet railways developed the express locomotive to its highest form; the P36, a 4-8-4 two-cylinder engine with 6ft diameter coupled wheels, of which 251 were built between 1950 and 1956. Further to the west, France had already excited astonishment with just one example of this wheel arrangement; a three-cylinder compound 242 A 1, considered to be the most powerful locomotive ever built in Europe. It was built in 1943, during the German occupation, by converting it from a 4-8-2. Its spiritual father was André Chapelon, arguably the most important twentieth-century steam locomotive engineer in the world. The imposing Spanish 242F, a 4-8-4 two-cylinder engine with 6ft 3in driving wheels from 1957, also deserves recognition. Admittedly, the fate of only ten examples went the tragic way of many other similar steam locomotives in an age of structural change. By 1974 there were none left in service, which was four years after the departure of the French 241 Ps and around the same time as the withdrawal of the Czech 498s.

Express trains in the late steam era

The end of the Berlin blockade on 12 May 1949 marked the change from the chaotic post-war situation to an equally controversial time when the two state systems were set up alongside one another. That same year, the Federal Republic of Germany (BRD) was founded in the West and the German Democratic Republic (DDR) was founded in the East. The four sectors of Berlin were set up independent of both countries and were subjected to complicated special conditions.

Tourist traffic developed in the East and West in quite opposite ways. In the West, cars were still very expensive at first, but motorbikes, affordable small cars and the legendary VW 'beetle' blossomed hugely in a wave of motorisation thanks to freely available fuel – energetically supported, of course, by the car industry, the oil economy and extremely well-meaning politicians.

Travel was an indispensable part of 'Prosperity for all' – the title of a book by the legendary Economics Minister, Ludwig Erhard. At the time of the Weimar Republic, employees had to beg their boss for even a single day's leave for family reasons, but now work contracts and pay agreements guaranteed ever more paid holidays. Now families travelled to the Black Forest or the Baltic Coast, to Upper Bavaria or the Harz Mountains, and a little later to the Austrian Tyrol and the Italian or Yugoslav Adriatic Coast. Meanwhile, the managing director (women were still rare in top positions) would attend very important meetings followed by a guys' night out in Munich, Bonn or Frankfurt, and as the autobahn network was still in its infancy and Alpine passes were not yet paved or even sealed, family holiday journeys were not recommended in the pre-war 'Adler', 'the Lloyd Alexander', the Fiat 500 or the Renault 4CV. And even if there was a well-maintained 'Maybach ', or BMW standing in the garage, the blue F-trains or red Ft services of the DB were quite simply faster for going on business trips. However, around 1955 the limited autobahn network started to expand rapidly, and at the same time a network of main roads and town bypasses was created. The purchasing power of German citizens also rose steadily. The 'DKW 3=6', the 'Opel Rekord', the 'Ford Taunus' or the 'Borgward Isabella' changed from being symbols of luxury to the everyday means of transport. As a result, customers began to desert the DB at an alarming speed.

Things looked significantly different in East Germany (DDR).

Automobile production and the condition of the road network lagged far behind demand, while fuel remained expensive and in short supply. The new elite in the body of the governing party, state, and the functionaries ruling the economy were just as dependent on the steam train as the rest of the working population, although those in power would have a holiday place in the Thuringer Forest, in the Erz Mountains or on the Baltic Coast. The availability of an EMW was the highest of privileges, while the owning of an IFA F8 was a constant challenge for the do-it-yourselfer.

Trains that travelled between the two zones retained a political, economic and emotional importance that should not be underestimated. They linked the Federal Republic with West Berlin; maintained family ties across the demarcation line and for a few days or weeks gave a glimpse into the living conditions in the competing systems. What is more, the inter-zonal trains were also often the means for people's final flight from East Germany, and after the Berlin Wall was built on 13 August 1961, no more permits to travel west were issued. However, in 1964 the authoritarian state granted this act of mercy to pensioners again.

The postal service had high economic and emotional priority for the inter-zonal trains. Every year between 30 and 50 million small parcels were sent 'over there', with coveted contents such as coffee, chocolate, little baked items, cigarettes, alcohol, preserved fruit, toys, and textiles – items that were all taken for granted in West Germany. Thefts by customs officers and Stasi agents were

routine. Just as important during this time of forbidden travel and an inadequate telephone network were the millions of letters that passed from Germany to Germany. So many silent feelings and quiet tears travelled in the postal van behind the hardworking 01.5 from Bebra towards the eastern border and from Erfurt to the west. In the run-up to Christmas, two postal vans were often needed.

Finally, the inter-zonal trains were an essential element of international East/West traffic. Behind the 01 or 03 rolled through coaches from Amsterdam, the Hook of Holland, Ostend, Paris, Lille, Basel and Rome to Warsaw, Brest and Moscow.

Rejuvenation in the prime of life: the 01 gets a new boiler

By 1955, many examples of the classic standard express locomotive class 01 had a quarter century of strenuous service behind them. Both the DB and DR decided to equip a proportion of their indispensable 01s with new boilers, but it was limited to those locomotives with bogie wheels of 3ft 3in diameter, from 01 102. After large-sale testing with the five 01s that had been equipped with combustion chambers and feedwater heaters in 1950, the DB decided to convert fifty members of the class. Like most of the new and rebuilt engines of the DB, they also received a steam operated regulator. The boilers were supplied by the Jung locomotive factory, the Engineering Workshop of Esslingen and the Nied Works, and the new-look locomotives appeared between May 1958 and December 1961. In the meantime, of course, electrification had taken great strides forward so

the operational demand for such powerful locomotives had already decreased. Enthusiasm for the rebuilt locomotives was limited, not least because of the successful upgrading of the old boilers of the 01s (and 03s). In this instance, all of the rivets had been replaced with welded seams, thereby significantly increasing their resistance to prolonged heavy working and their flexibility to cope with temperature and pressure fluctuations. The first converted 01s were withdrawn as early as 1967.

With the DR, the position of the boiler was much more critical for a number of different reasons. When the renovations at the DB had already been completed, thirty-five machines were taken to the Meiningen Works and between April 1962 and May 1965 were equipped with all-welded boilers with combustion chambers. With their raised boiler position, a pointed smokebox door, a general streamlining of the fittings and some fitted with Boxpok wheels, their appearance changed much more than that of the DB rebuilds. They were also renumbered 01 501 – 535. In accordance with the economic situation, this class of locomotives remained in service until 1977 and were mostly used in intensive express train working until they were completely phased out by 1982. A small historical irony is that the proud 01.5, a valuable symbol of the socialist self-sufficiency of East Germany, solved the major travel needs for the West Germans in the divided Germany's operational history like no other locomotive type, mainly due to its use on the connections from Berlin with the border towns of Probstzella, Bebra, Helmstedt and Hamburg.

01 149 with new boiler
Fifty examples of the two-cylinder 01 had the pleasure of the new boilers. Nuremberg's 01 149 on an East – West transit in 1966 is hauling a set of modern Czech coaches. (*Gottfried Turnwald*)

An express on the DR
From an elevated vantage point, 01 513 is seen with a typical DR express of the 1960s, made up of pre-war coaches passing through Bad Kösen. (*Gerhard Illner*)

Inter-zonal traffic
The Erfurt 01.5s were responsible for the inter-zonal and Berlin traffic to Bebra until 1973. 01 520 is seen leaving the Hönebach Tunnel a few miles west of the internal German border in March 1972. A friendly wave from the fireman for the photographer and an imposing oil-smoke effect combine to make a fabulous picture! (*Andreas Knipping*)

Unlucky locomotive

In addition to 03 2237, which was modernised with a boiler from a withdrawn class 22, the similarly coal-fired 01 1516 stands ready for departure in Dresden-Neustadt (New Town) on 29 January 1977. That same year, its boiler exploded as the result of an inexplicable oversight and the neglection of duty by the driver and fireman. (*Miroslav Petr*)

Boxpok wheels

01 502 displays an almost futuristic impression with the streamlining at the top of the boiler from smokebox to cab, seen here at Bebra on 18 July 1964. The later construction features of the 01 fell victim to the early dismantling of the original version. (*Peter Konzelmann*)

18 201 and 18 314: two engines from fairyland

The East German Reichsbahn retained a 120kph (75mph) 'limit' due to political decisions. However, in order to test passenger coaches for the competitive export market, the DR needed a number of vehicles capable of 150kph (93mph). Max Baumberg, the director of the research and development centre at Halle, managed to achieve two ingenious conversions. The 40-year-old

Baden IV h 18 314 was extensively modernised in 1960, the core of the conversion being a welded boiler of the same design as that used for the 03.10s, 22s and 41s. Externally it was more attractive than the DB class 10 because of the streamlining around the cylinders and front. It was painted green, which further underlined the specialness of this unique locomotive. And that was not all: the DR had at its disposal the streamlined tank engine 61 002 with 7ft 6in driving wheels.

No one had been able to do much with it and so its excellent running gear and motion became the basis of another high-speed test locomotive. The freight locomotive 45 024 provided the outside cylinders, and the steam producer was the same new boiler as on the 18 314. With this, the DR created the fastest steam locomotive in the world after 1945, and it remains so to this today. Once again, elegant streamlining and green livery ensured the memorable appearance of 18 201. It was put into intensive trials in 1961 and on 12 October 1972, the driver Rindelhardt was given special permission to accelerate to 182.4 kph (114mph). As in the days of the 05 before the war, such high-speed runs with steam locomotives were far from simple. The braking process in particular, which extended over many miles, required a great deal of sensitivity and judgement in order to avoid damaging the valuable technology. Nevertheless, glowing sparks from the brake-blocks flew far over the locomotive. Even if many steam locomotive enthusiasts do not like to admit it, worldwide experience proved that steam operation at around 85 – 90mph results in very hard-to-cross limits.

Left and below:
18 314 – a rebuild for the locomotive research centre at Halle
A high point in the framework of the successful 'Reko' boiler project was the toughening up of the 40-year-old 18 314 as a high-speed test locomotive in the service of rolling stock exports. Its inclusion in regular express passenger work often occurred after its rebuilding in December 1960 until December 1971.

Superlative steam locomotive

The 'Reko' programme was a genuine marvel with the wonderful reconstruction of 18 201, certainly the most remarkable creation of German steam locomotive building since the war. Since then it has spent more than two thirds of its life in special services for railway enthusiasts. (*Andreas Knipping*)

When 02 0201 was in service

The idea of the '*Plandampf*' helped 18 201 (now renumbered 02 0201) perform on regular expresses, such as between Saalfeld and Probstzella. It undertook the timetable of the diesel engines on this single unelectrified track – seen here in 1992 – without any effort.

The last oil-firing: a huge gain in performance

Right at the start of our overview was the change from wood to coal, with its higher energy efficiency acting as the 'big bang' of the industrial revolution, and thus signalling the start of the railway age, too. The Second World War, with its huge fleets of tanks, trucks and aircraft, brought the much more efficient and flexible fuel, oil, in an offensive that continues today. The domination of diesel locomotives and multiple units began on the railway networks of the world. Together with electrification that began after the First World War, the end of the steam locomotive was in sight. The conversion of the entire fleet was a technological, and in hindsight a financial, project for an entire generation. Several railway administrations decided on a transitional period to convert the newest steam locomotives to oil firing, which was necessary, indeed essential on some lines, as the steam production required was very difficult or even beyond the capacity of a human fireman stoking with coal. In terms of social history, we must not neglect the fact that from 1949 onwards, better working conditions were given more prominence in the media and in legislation. A new generation of employees rebelled against excessive working conditions, and good firemen found increasingly easier jobs outside the railway. Firstly, the DB converted a number of their new boiler 01.10s as well as some of classes 41 and 44 and the two new class 10s to firing with a light oil. The rebuilding consisted of a removal of the grate, ashpan and spark-arrester and the lower

outside wall of the firebox and the introduction of an oil container in the former coal space of the tender and installation of the oil burners in the front of the lower firebox wall. Thirty-four examples of the 01.10s were rebuilt in this way by Henschel between July 1956 and June 1958, and these and the class 10s were – and remained – the most powerful and efficient steam engines ever used in Germany.

A few years later the DR also went over to oil-firing for steam traction required on those routes demanding the highest performance, although they used a heavier oil that was available almost as a by-product of the nationally owned mineral oil industry. The reconstructed 01s with the numbers 519–535 went into service out of the Meiningen Works with oil-firing between February 1964 and May 1965, and were primarily used on international services between Berlin and the DB border points of Bebra and Hamburg-Altona. A further eleven of the 01s that had already been rebuilt as 01.5s were converted to oil-burning in the same way between February 1965 and April 1966, so that only seven coal-fired 01.5s remained. Between June 1965 and September 1972 seventeen examples of class 03.10 also left Meiningen Works after being overhauled for oil-burning.

We are dealing here with an era in which the leaders of both the Soviet Union and East Germany thoughtlessly put in place an economic future dependent on oil and nuclear energy. The electrification of the railway was ruthlessly stopped; huge numbers of imported diesel locomotives from the Soviet Union would replace the

remaining steam locomotives. It is unsurprising that the outstanding test locomotives at the Halle Research Centre, namely 18 201 (rebuilt from 61 002), 18 314 (the rebuilt Baden IV h) and 19 015 and 19 022 (rebuilt Saxon XX HV 2-8-2s) were also converted to oil-firing in 1967/1968.

After almost exactly a century, all German steam locomotive development ceased in the late 1960s, even though they remained in traffic for a further decade.

A quick farewell on the DB

In the mid-1950s, the German Federal Minister of Transport and the main administration of the DB made the decision to replace steam traction over a twenty-year period. Electrification would initially be installed on the most heavily trafficked routes, while diesel could be introduced quickly on other lesser routes and branches. Using both of these systems, the areas of steam operation could be brought to an end in a pincer movement. The programme was implemented according to plan and naturally affected express train haulage at an early stage, although steam operation remained longer on slower trains and on goods traffic on heavily used lines. A 'knock-out' blow was the electrification of the north-south line from Hanover to Würzburg and Frankfurt am Main in 1963.

Nowhere else in Germany had steam locomotives been pressed so hard as on this main line. For the class 18.6s and 03.10s, on which money had been lavishly spent on their reboilering, there were few diagrams possible from 1965/1966 onwards. Many 01s and 03s were stored at the same time and then withdrawn. When the Osnabrück – Bremen – Hamburg and the Hamm – Minden – Hanover lines were electrified in 1968, the era of steam-hauled expresses on the DB was nearly at an end. Although there were still some large-wheeled steam locomotives active, such as the 003s (ex 03) in north Germany, the Rhineland and in the end between Ulm and Friedrichshafen, they almost only ran on semi-fast and stopping services. The late express steam areas were:

- 001 (ex 01): Trier – Koblenz (until 1972), Hof – Regensburg (until 1971), Hof – Bamberg (until 1973)
- 011 (ex 01.10 coal-fired): Rheine – Emden (until 1973)
- 012 (ex 01.10 oil-fired): Hamburg – Westerland (until 1972), Rheine – Emden (until 1975).

A slow farewell on the DR

Much more complicated was the departure of steam from train haulage and even express train work in both the German Democratic Republic (DDR) and in Berlin itself. The diesel locomotives imported from the Soviet Union proved to be susceptible to damage and could hardly match the performance of the powerful and modern steam engines. The coal-fired 01.20s (ex 01) and 01.15s (ex 01.5s) remained on the high-speed Berlin – Dresden route until 1977. The 01.15s and the 03.20s (ex 03) remained on the Leipzig – Berlin line, including some express work, until 1979. The 03.20s were kept lastly on the Berlin – Szczecin route (until 1975) and Dresden – Cottbus/Görlitz until 1978. 27 November 1977 was a black day for late steam traction in Germany when the boiler of 01 1516, the train engine of D 567, exploded during a stop at Bitterfeld. Seven people were killed and fifty-nine were wounded. The subsequent inquiry revealed that the cause was the most serious operating error of a steam locomotive crew, namely the failure to keep a watch on the water level in the boiler. Neither the driver nor the fireman could be questioned.

In 1979 the economy of East Germany suffered a massive setback due to a steep rise in the price of oil set by the Soviet Union. Suddenly, electrification came back into consideration and coal-fired steam engines were treasured, while diesel and oil-fired steam locomotives became an economic issue. Coal-fired 01.15s and 01.20s were brought back into steam and put in service between Magdeburg and Berlin in 1982. The most ambitious turns for express steam locomotives in the late 1970s was between Stralsund and Berlin with the oil-fired 03.00s (ex 03.10). In the summer of 1977, the engines averaged 767km (480 miles) per day in a seven-day period. In the winter of 1978/1979, which was marked by unprecedented cold weather and snow off the Baltic Sea, the service was reduced to four days of 535km (335 miles). In the summer of 1979, three-day timetables were restored averaging 598km (374 miles). This spectacular operation ceased at the end of May 1980. All that remained was the single operation of oil-burning 01.5s on the Saalfeld – Camburg line and occasionally on the international Probstzella – Berlin trains until 1982. The operation of expresses with steam traction, a remarkable chapter in the national history of technology and economics, came to an end with little celebration and no media attention.

However, the express steam locomotive was not dead. Both the DB and DR and, above all, a number of private enterprises run by enthusiasts, saved a large number of machines from the cutting torch and brought back to life and into operation a number of decrepit locomotive hulks. Now, almost four decades after the last regular steam services, people can travel on astonishing train journeys with locomotives of the past.

APPENDICES

Operation sections 1955

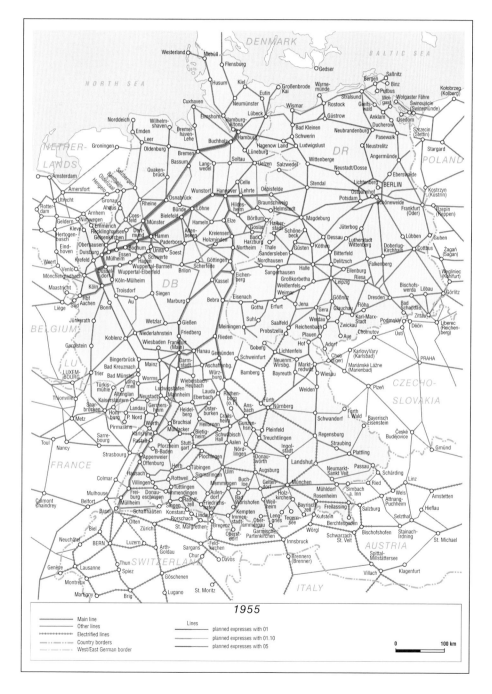

1955

Main line	
Other lines	
Electrified lines	
Country borders	
West/East German border	

Lines
- planned expresses with 01
- planned expresses with 01.10
- planned expresses with 05

0   100 km

The reign of the steam locomotive between Basel and Westerland was still unbroken in 1955. In both parts of Germany, classes 23, 39 and 41 played a significant role in local passenger and freight work. Whereas the DB had electric traction on important routes in Bavaria and Württemberg, the change to alternating current electrification began very modestly in the DR with the section from Halle to Köthen.

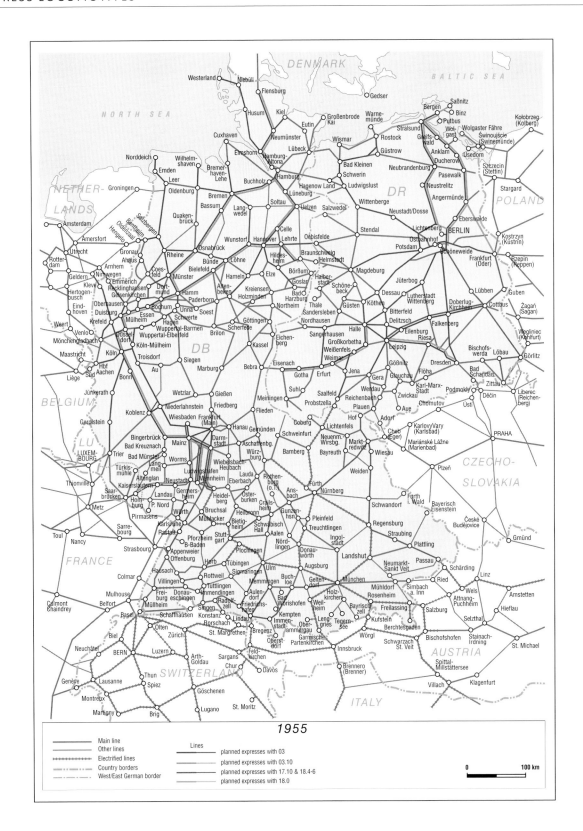

1955

	Lines
Main line	planned expresses with 03
Other lines	planned expresses with 03.10
Electrified lines	planned expresses with 17.10 & 18.4-6
Country borders	planned expresses with 18.0
West/East German border	

0   100 km

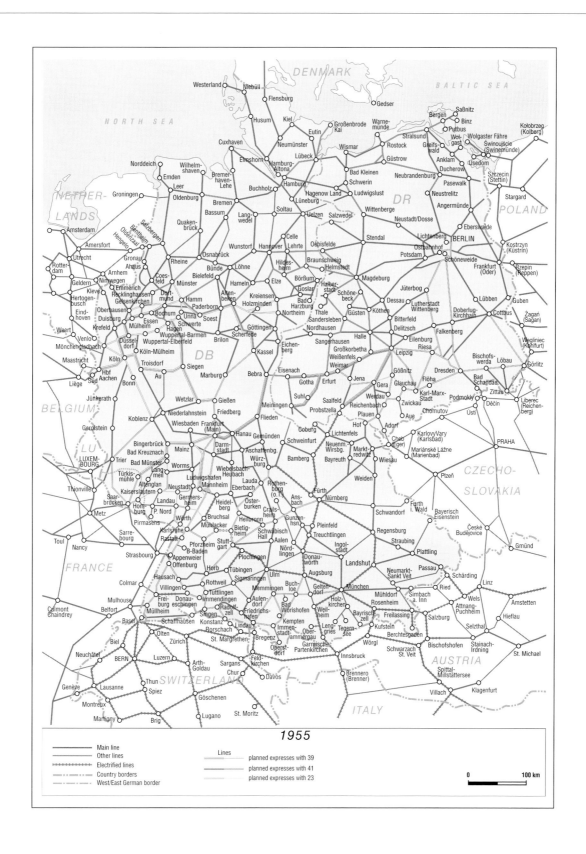

1955

Main line
Other lines
Electrified lines
Country borders
West/East German border

Lines
planned expresses with 39
planned expresses with 41
planned expresses with 23

0   100 km

Operation sections 1961

A great deal has changed for the DB in 1961 when compared with 1955, to the detriment of the steam locomotive. The section from Basel to Passau and up into the Ruhr had been electrified. Express train haulage with steam was now very restricted in Baden-Württemberg and southern Bavaria. The next epoch-making changes are still to come – electric traction from Würzburg and Frankfurt to Hanover in 1963, to Bremen in 1964, and Hamburg in 1965. Developments in the DR are more modest. The small, electrified network between Magdeburg, Leipzig and Weissenfels, which was rebuilt in 1955 having been dismantled in 1946, did not necessarily mean that steam haulage from Rügen in the north to the Saale and Elbe Valleys in the south was unwanted.

1961

Main line	Lines
Other lines	planned expresses with 01
Electrified lines	planned expresses with 01.10
Country borders	planned expresses with 10
West/East German border	0 100 km

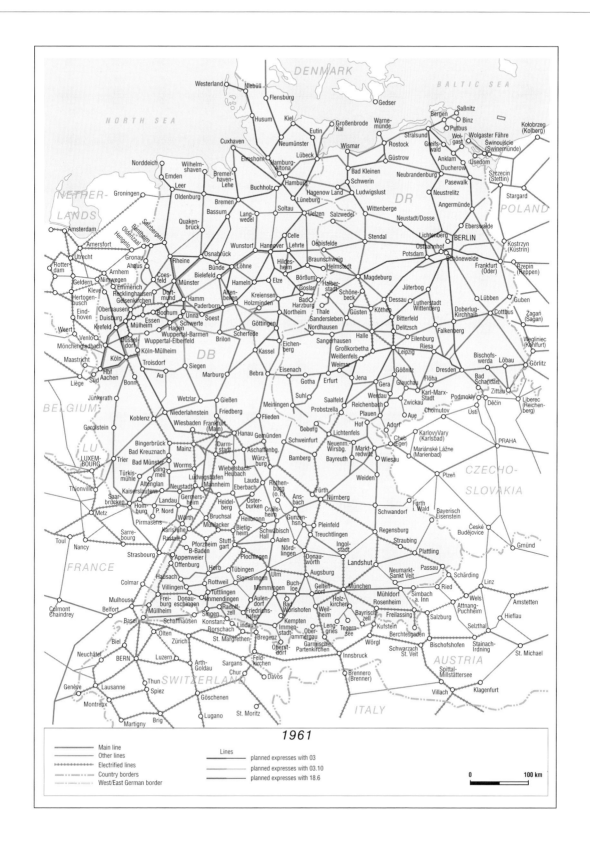

1961

————	Main line
————	Other lines
+++++++	Electrified lines
————	Country borders
·········	West/East German border

Lines

————	planned expresses with 03
————	planned expresses with 03.10
————	planned expresses with 18.6

0   100 km

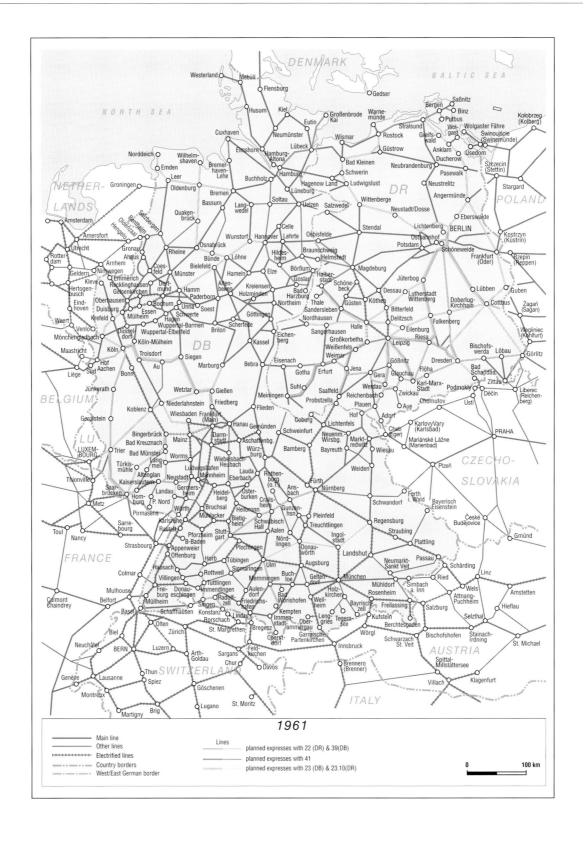

1961

Main line		
Other lines		
Electrified lines		
Country borders		
West/East German border		

Lines

planned expresses with 22 (DR) & 39(DB)

planned expresses with 41

planned expresses with 23 (DB) & 23.10(DR)

0   100 km

An overview of express steam locomotives procured by the former regional state railways
The information is definitive at the time of being taken into traffic without taking account of any subsequent rebuilding

North German State Railway classes

Class	Built	DR No.	Type	Number	Driving wheel diameter	Max speed mph	Weight without tender (tons)	Boiler pressure lbs psi	Heating surface (sq ft)	Heating surface superheater (sq ft)	No. of tender axles	Water capacity (gallons) (most frequent)	Coal capacity (tons)
pr S 1 Han	1884–1887	–	1B n2v	14	1.869	100	39	12	98	–	3	12	5/7
pr S 1	1885–1898	–	1B n2	260	1.980	90	41,3	12	93,95	–	3	12	5/7
pr S 2	1890/91	–	2B n2v	4	1.980	100	45,2	12	117,8	–	3	15	5
pr S 2	1892	–	2B n2	148	1.980	100	49	12	124,8	–	3	15	5
pr S 2 Wellrohrkessel	1892	–	2B n2v	1	1.960	100	51,5	14	104.15	–	3	15	5
pr S 3	1893–1904	13⁰	2B n2v	1.027	1.980	100	50,4	12	117,8	–	3	15	5
pr S 5 Grafenstaden	1894, 1902/03	–	2B n4v	23	1.980	100	54	14	110	–	4	21,5	5/7
pr S 4	1898–1909	13⁵	2B h2v	107	1.980	100	55	12	100,7/104,5	30,7/33,9	4	16	5
pr S 5¹ Hannover	1900–1903	–	2B n4v	17	1.980	100	56,7	14	100	–	4	21,5	5/7
pr S 7 Hannover	1902–1906	–	2B1 n4v	159	1.980	100	62,9	14	163	–	4	30	6,5
pr S 7 Grafenstaden	1902–1905	–	2B1n4v	79	1.980	110	65	14/15/16	177/178	–	4	30	6,5
pr S 9 Kuhn/ Wittfeld	1904	–	2B2 n3v	2	2.200	130	89,5	14	260	–	4	31,5	7
pr S 5²	1905–1911	–	2B n2v	367	1.980	100	55,2	12	136,89	–	4	21,5	5/7
pr S 6	1906–1913	13¹⁰	2B h2	584	2.100	110	60,7	12	136,9	40,3	4	21,5	7
pr S 9 Hannover	1908–1910	14⁰	2B1 n4v	99	1.980	110	74,5	14	229,71	–	4	31,5	7
pr S 10	1910–1914	17⁰	2C h4	202	1.980	110	79,5	12	154,6	52,9	4	31,5	7
pr S 10¹ 1911	1911–1914	17¹⁰	2C h4v	145	1.980	110	82,2	15	165,5	52,1	4	31,5	7
pr S 10¹ 1914	1914–1916	17¹⁰	2C h4v	92	1.980	110	84,1	15	163	58,5	4	31,5	7
pr S 10²	1914–1916	17²	2C h3	124	1.980	110	79,9	14	153	61,5	4	31,5	7
pr S 11	1918	–	1C2 h4v	7	2.140	100	88,7	16	182,9	55	4	27	8
EL P 3	1892	–	2B n2v	1	1.850	90	47,8	12	113,6	–	3	?	?
EL P 3	1894	–	2B n2	8	1.850	90	47,8	12	125	–	3	15	5
EL P 4	1895	–	2B n2v	6	1.850	90	47,9	12	125	–	3	15	5
EL S 3	1900/01	–	2B n2v	40	1.980	100	54	12	117,8	–	3	15	5
EL S 5	1902–1913	–	2B n4v	54	1.980	90	54	15	170	–	4	18	5
EL P 7	1902–1913	–	2C n4v	30	1.850	95	65,8	16	209	–	4	20	5
EL S 9	1906–1909	–	2C n4v	80	1.980	100	67,1	16	209	–	4	20	5
EL S 12	1909	–	2C1 h4v	8	2.040	100	82,2	15	200,2	38,5	4	21	6
EL S 10¹	1913–1915	–	2C h4v	17	1.980	110	82/84	15	165,5	52,1	4	31,5	7

Class	Built	DR No.	Type	Number	Driving wheel diameter	Max speed mph	Weight without tender (tons)	Boiler pressure lbs psi	Heating surface (sq ft)	Heating surface superheater (sq ft)	No. of tender axles	Water capacity (gallons) (most frequent)	Coal capacity (tons)
meck	1864–1869	–	1B n2	20	1.820	?	?	7,3/8,7	?	–	3	?	?
old S 3	1903/04	13[18]	2B n2v	6	1.980	95	52,2	12	119,4	–	4	20	5
old S 5[2]	1909–1913	13[18]	2B n2v	11	1.980	100	53,4	12	140,7	–	4	20	5
old S 10	1917	16[0]	1C1 h2	3	1.980	100	73,9	14	145,8	41	4	20	5
LBE S 5	1907–1911	13[0]	2B n2v	7	1.980	100	54,1	12	141,6	–	3	12	5
LBE S 10	1912	17[1]	2C h4	5	1.980	110	71,7	12	143,7	42,2	3	16	5
LBE S 10[2]	1913–1932	17[3]	2C h3	10	1.980	110	78	14	141,1	53	3	16	5

Note:
Pr = Prussian State Railway
EL = Alsace-Lorraine State Railway
meck = Mecklenburg State Railway
old = Oldenburg State Railway
LBE = Lübeck-Büchen State Railway

Bavarian State Railway classes

Class	Built	DR No.	Type	Number	Driving wheel diameter	Max speed mph	Weight without tender (tons)	Boiler pressure lbs psi	Heating surface (sq ft)	Heating surface superheater (sq ft)	No. of tender axles	Water capacity (gallons) (most frequent)	Coal capacity (tons)
Ostbahn A	1857/58		2A n2	12	1.828	?		6	83	–	3	7	4
Ostbahn A	1849	–	1A1 n2	12	1.828	?		6	80	–	3	7	4
Ostbahn B	1872/1875	–	1B n2	6	1.835	?		8/9	84/90	–	3	8,5	6
bay B IX	1874–1887	–	1B n2	104	1.870	90	33,6	10	87,7	–	3	10,5	5
bay B X	1890/91	–	1B n2v	14	1.870	90	43	12	99	–	3	12	5
bay B XI$_{ZW}$	1892/93	–	2B n2	39	1.870	90	50,4	12	116,2	–	4	18	6,5
bay B XI$_{VERB}$	1892–1900	–	2B n2v	100	1.870	90	51	13	116,8	–	4	18	6,5
bay AA I	1896	–	2aA1 n2v	1	1.860	90	51,5	13	116,8	–	3	14	5
bay C V	1899–1901	17[3]	2C n4v	42	1.870	90	66,2	14	153	–	4	21	7
bay S 2/5$_{VAUCL}$	1901	–	2B1 n4v	2	1.829	90	62,8	14	207,4	–	4	20,8	6
bay S 3/5 N	1903–1907	17[4]	2C n4v	39	1.870	110	69,3	14	210,5	–	4	21	7
bay S 2/5	1904	14[1]	2B1 n4v	10	2.000	110	68,6	16	205,5	–	4	21	7
bay S 3/5 H	1906–1911	17[5]	2C h4v	30	1.870	110	71,9	16	159,5	33,9	4	21,8	7,5
bay S 2/6	1906	15[0]	2B2 h4v	1	2.200	150	83,4	14	214,5	38	4	26	8
bay S 3/6 a, b, c, f	1908–1914	18[4]	2C1 h4v	26	1.870	120	88,3	15	218,4	50	4	26,4	7,5/8
bay S 3/6 d, e	1912	18[4]	2C1 h4v	18	2.000	120	91,6	15	219,1	50	4	32,5	8
bay S 3/6 h, i	1914–1918	18[4]	2C1 h4v	35	1.870	120	92,3	15	219	55,6	4	26,4	8
bay S 3/6 k	1923/24	18[4-5]	2C1 h4v	30	1.870	120	94	15	215	62	4	26,4/27,4	8,5

Class	Built	DR No.	Type	Number	Driving wheel diameter	Max speed mph	Weight without tender (tons)	Boiler pressure lbs psi	Heating surface (sq ft)	Heating surface superheater (sq ft)	No. of tender axles	Water capacity (gallons) (most frequent)	Coal capacity (tons)
bay S 3/6 l, m, n, o	1926–1930	18[5]	2C1 h4v	40	1.870	120	94,7-96,2	16	218,4	76,3	4	27,4/31,7	8,5
pfälz. (Namen)	1853–1864	–	2A n2	18	1.830	75	24,2	6,2–7,3	68,6–78,5	–	3	5,7	3,2
pfälz P 1II	1876	–	1B n2	6	1.855	90	34,8	10	78,4	–	2	7,5	3,5
pfälz P 1III	1880–1884	–	1B n2	9	1.855	90	34,3	10	79,2	–	3	10	3,8
pfälz P 2I	1891–1896	–	1B1 n2	22	1.855	90	47,7	12	92,2/106,8	–	3	12/14	4,7
pfälz P 3I	1898–1904	14[1]	2B1 n2	12	1.980	100	59,6	13	168,2/171,3	–	3	16	6
pfälz P 3II	1900	–	2aB1 n2v	1	1.870	90	68	14	192,5	–	4	20	6,5
pfälz P 4	1905/06	–	2B1 n4v	11	2.010	120	74,3	15	181,3/223	–	4	20	6,5
pfälz S 3/6 g	1914	18[4]	2C1 h4v	10	1.870	120	89,7	15	219	55,6	4	26,4	8

Note:

Ostbahn = Eastern Railway

bay = Bavarian State Railway

pfälz = Palatinate State Railway

Types: 2A = 4-2-0; 1A1=2-2-2: 1B = 2-4-0: 2B = 4-4-0: 2B1 = 4-4-2: 2C=4-6-0: 2C1=4-6-2: n=saturated h = superheated 2 = 2 cylinders etc: v = compound

Driving wheel diameter conversion: 5ft = 1.52m: 6ft = 1.83m: 7ft = 2.13m

Max Speed: 90kph = 56 mph: 100kph = 62.5 mph: 110kph = 69 mph: 120kph = 75 mph: 130kph = 81.25 mph: 140kph = 87.5 mph: 150kph = 93.75 mph:
175kph = 109.375 mph

Boiler pressure: 10 bar = 142 lbs psi: 15 bar = 213 lbs psi : 20 bar = 284 lbs psi

Heating surface: 1 sq m = 10.56 sq ft: 100 sq m = 1,056 sq ft: 200 sq m = 2,112 sq ft

Water capacity: 1 m cubed = 220 gal. (approx) 20m3 = 4,400 gal., 30m3 = 6,600 gal.

State Railway of Saxony

Class	Built	DR No.	Type	Number	Driving wheel diameter	Max speed mph	Weight without tender (tons)	Boiler pressure lbs psi	Heating surface (sq ft)	Heating surface superheater (sq ft)	No. of tender axles	Water capacity (gallons) (most frequent)	Coal capacity (tons)
sä VI a	1856–1868	–	1A1 n2	31	1.830	?	30	7/7,5	85,9-87,1	–	2	?	?
sä VI	1860–1870	–	1B n2	41	1.830	85	32,5	8,5	83,9	–	2	?	?
sä VIII1	1870	–	2B n2	8	1.830	70	36,8	8,5	93,2	–	3	12	5
sä VI b V	1886–1890	–	1B n2v	14	1.875	85	43,2	12	102	–	3	12	5
sä VIII2	1891/1894	13[70]	2B n2	20	1.875	85	49,4	10/12	123,5/121,6	–	4	16	5
sä VIII V1	1896/97	13[71]	2B n2v	20	1.885	85	54,3	12	117,5	–	4	18	5
sä VIII V1	1900	13[15]	2B n2v	12	1.885	90	56,8	12	129	–	4	18	5
sä X V	1900–1903	14[2]	2B1 n4v	15	1.980	120	69,3	15	160,8	–	4	18	5
sä X H1	1909–1913	14[3]	2B1 h2	18	1.980	100	70,1	12	171,7	47,1	4	18	5
sä XII H	1906	17[6]	2C h4	6	1.885	100	73,3	12	146,1	43,8	4	21	7
sä XII HV	1908–1914	17[7]	2C h4v	42	1.905	100	78,3	15	146,3	41	4	21	7
sä XII H1	1909	17[8]	2C h2	7	1.885	100	72,7	12	177,7	47,1	4	21	7
sä XVIII H	1917/18	18[0]	2C1'h3	10	1.905	100	93,5	14	215,8	72	4	31	6
sä XX HV	1918–1923	19[0]	1D1 h4v	23	1.905	100	99,9	15	227	74	4	31	6

Note: sä = Saxony

Württemberg State Railway

Class	Built	DR No.	Type	Number	Driving wheel diameter	Max speed mph	Weight without tender (tons)	Boiler pressure lbs psi	Heating surface (sq ft)	Heating surface superheater (sq ft)	No. of tender axles	Water capacity (gallons) (most frequent)	Coal capacity (tons)
VI	1854	–	2B n2	6	1.842	?	27,8	7	67,8	–	2	10	6
A	1858–1860	–	2B n2	6	1.842	?	27,8	7	67,8	–	2	10	6
B	1865–1868	–	2B n2	6	1.842	?	33	9	100,1	–	2	10	6
AD	1899–1907	13^{16}	2B n2v	98	1.800	100	45	14	129	–	3	15,5	5
ADh	1907–1909	13^{17}	2B h2	17	1.800	100	46,3	12	135,9	31,3	3	15,5	5
C	1909–1921	18^{1}	2C1 h4v	41	1.800	120	76,3	15	261/273	53/65	4	20/30	6/10

Baden State Railway

Class	Built	DR No.	Type	Number	Driving wheel diameter	Max speed mph	Weight without tender (tons)	Boiler pressure lbs psi	Heating surface (sq ft)	Heating surface superheater (sq ft)	No. of tender axles	Water capacity (gallons) (most frequent)	Coal capacity (tons)
III a/b/c	1844/45	–	1A1	22	1.830	?	19/20	5,3	63/76	–	3	5,4	3,5
VIII	1847/48	–	1A1	9	1.830	?	21	6	63,7	–	3	5,4	3,5
I c	1856	–	2A n2	3	1.890	47	25,2	7	74,2	–	2	5,1	?
IX	1854–1863	–	2A n2	18	2.134	46	27,9	7	82,8	–	3	5,4	?
III a	1861–1875	–	2B n2	90	1.830	60	31,6	8/9	81,5/82,9	–	2	5,7-8	?
II a	1888–1890	–	2B n2	24	1.860	90	45,4	10	119	–	3	11/12	?
II b	1891	–	2B n2	10	1.860	90	46,9	10	121,5	–	3	12	?
II c	1892–1900	–	2B n2	35	2.100	90	45,7	12	102,6	–	4	15	5
II d	1902/05	–	2B1 n4v	18	2100	110	75,7	16	210	–	4	20	7
IV f	1907–1912	18^{2}	2C1 h4v	35	1.800	100	88,3	16	208,7	50	4	20	7
IV h	1918–1920	18^{3}	2C1 h4v	20	2.100	140	96,9	15	224,8	77,6	4	29,5	9

Last Prussian mixed traffic locomotive significant for express work

Class	Built	DR No.	Type	Number	Driving wheel diameter	Max speed mph	Weight without tender (tons)	Boiler pressure lbs psi	Heating surface (sq ft)	Heating surface superheater (sq ft)	No. of tender axles	Water capacity (gallons) (most frequent)	Coal capacity (tons)
P 10	1922–1927	39	1D1 h3	260	1.750	110	?	14	217	82	4	31,5	7

Express steam locomotives built or rebuilt by the Reichsbahn and Bundesbahn and also relevant mixed traffic and freight engines used on express work

The information is definitive at the time of being taken into traffic without taking account of any subsequent rebuilding

German State Railway 1920 – 1945

Class	DR No.	DR No.	Built	Type	Number	Driving wheel diameter	Max speed mph	Weight without tender (tons)	Boiler pressure lbs psi	Heating surface (sq ft)	Heating surface superheater (sq ft)	No. of tender axles	Water capacity (most frequent)	Coal capacity (gallons) (tons)
02	–	–	1925/26	2C1 h4v	10	2.000	130	16	113	238	100	4	32	10
01	001	01.20	1926–1938	2C1 h2	240	2.000	120/130	16	109/111	238/247	100/85	4	34	10
03	003	03.20	1930–1937	2C1 h2	298	2.000	130/140	16	99/103	202,2/203,6	70/72,2	4	34	10

Class	DR No.	DR No.	Built	Type	Number	Driving wheel diameter	Max speed mph	Weight without tender (tons)	Boiler pressure lbs psi	Heating surface (sq ft)	Heating surface superheater (sq ft)	No. of tender axles	Water capacity (most frequent)	Coal capacity (gallons) (tons)
04	–	–	1932	2C1 h4v	2	2.000	130	25	109	188,6/206,8	88/85,6	4	32	10
05	–	–	1935	2C2 h3	2	2.300	175	20	130	256	90	5	37	10
61	–	–	1935	2C2 h2t	1	2300	175	20	129	152	69,2	–	17	5
41	041	41	1936–1940	1D1 h2	366	1.600	90	16	102	203,1	72,2	4	30/32/34	10
05	–	–	1937	2C2 h3 (Kst)	1	2.300	175	20	125	228	82	5	35	10
06	–	–	1939	2D2 h3	2	2.000	140	20	142	289	132,5	5	38	10
61	–	–	1939	2C3 h3t	1	2300	175	20	146	150	69,2	–	21	6
01[10]	011/012	–	1939/40	2C1 h3	55	2.000	150	16	114	246,9	86	5	38	10
03[10]	–	03.00	1939/40	2C1 h3	60	2.000	150	16	103	203,4	72,2	4	34	10
19[10]	–	–	1941	1Do1 h8	1	1.250	175	20	110	240	109,9	5	37	10

German Federal Railway

Class	DR No.	DR No.	Built	Type	Number	Driving wheel diameter	Max speed mph	Weight without tender (tons)	Boiler pressure lbs psi	Heating surface (sq ft)	Heating surface superheater (sq ft)	No. of tender axles	Water capacity (most frequent)	Coal capacity (gallons) (tons)
23	023	–	1950–1959	1C1 h2	105	1.750	110	16	82,8	156,3	73,8	4	31	8
10	–	–	1957	2C1 h3	2	2.000	140	18	119	216,4	105,7	4	40	12,5

(East) German State Railway after 1945

Class	DR No.	DR No.	Built	Type	Number	Driving wheel diameter	Max speed mph	Weight without tender (tons)	Boiler pressure lbs psi	Heating surface (sq ft)	Heating surface superheater (sq ft)	No. of tender axles	Water capacity (most frequent)	Coal capacity (gallons) (tons)
23[10]	–	35	1956–1959	1C1 h2	113	1.750	110	16	110	159,6	68,5	4	28	7

Major rebuilds DB and DR 1953 – 1965
German Federal Railway

Class	DR No.	DR No.	Built	Type	Number	Driving wheel diameter	Max speed mph	Weight without tender (tons)	Boiler pressure lbs psi	Heating surface (sq ft)	Heating surface superheater (sq ft)	No. of tender axles	Water capacity (most frequent)	Coal capacity (gallons) (tons)
01	001	–	1958–1961	2C1 h2	50	2.000	130	16	108,3	193	100	4	34	10
01[10]	011/012	–	1953–1956	2C1 h3	54	2.000	140	16	110,8	206,5	96,1	5	38	10
03[10]	–	–	1953–1956	2C1 h3	25	2.000	140	16	104,2	177,5	95,8	4	34	10
18[5] > 18[6]	–	–	1953–1956	2C1 h4v	30	1.870	120	16	100,3	195	72	4	31,7	9

(East) German State Railway

Class	DR No.	DR No.	Built	Type	Number	Driving wheel diameter	Max speed mph	Weight without tender (tons)	Boiler pressure lbs psi	Heating surface (sq ft)	Heating surface superheater (sq ft)	No. of tender axles	Water capacity (most frequent)	Coal capacity (gallons) (tons)
01 > 01[5]	–	01.05/15	1962–1965	2C1 h2	35	2.000	130	16	111	224,5	97,5	4	34	10
03	–	03.20	1969–1975	2C1 h2	52	2.000	130	16	101	206,3	83,8	4	34	10
03[10]	–	03.00/10	1959	2C1 h3	16	2.000	140	16	104	206,3	83,8	4	34	10
61 > 18	–	02.00	1961	2C1 h3	1	2.300	175	16	113,6	206,3	83,8	4	34	10
18 314	–	02.00	1961	2C1 h4v	1	2.100	150	16	105	199,5	80	4	34	10
19	–	04	1964/65	1D1 h4v	2	1.905	120	16	107,7	206,3	83,8	4/5	34/38	10
39 > 22	–	39	1958–1962	1D1 h3	85	1.750	110	16	107,5	206,3	83,6	4	34	10

It was once really modern

The Bavarian S 3/5 was built in the transition time of 1900 to modern principles, with four-cylinder compound drive, high-pitched boiler and bar frames, although it was still without superheating. The author once heard the tale of a driver who was born in 1898, remembering his journey as a young fireman in 1925 with such a locomotive from Munich to Lindau, when it was a replacement for a failed S 3/6. Thanks to his firing skill, the train arrived punctually at its destination. The history of steam locomotive operation has always been about the hard, self-sacrificing work of the crews and mechanics involved.